Colour In Your Thinking..

FINDING the REAL YOU

A Practical Guide For Students

By Cathy Dean

Cathy Dean

Finding the Real You
A Practical Guide for Students

© Cathy Dean

ISBN: 978-1906316-73-0

All rights reserved

Published in 2010 by HotHive Books, Evesham, UK
www.thehothive.com

The right of Cathy Dean to be identified as the author of this work has been asserted by her in accordance with the Copyright, Designs and Patents Act 1988.

A CIP record of this book is available from the British Library.

No part of this publication may be reproduced in any form or by any means without prior permission from the author.

Printed in the UK by TJ International, Padstow

For Michelle, thank you for inspiring me

Contents

About the author — 7

Introduction — 9

Chapter 1: This is me… I think? — 13

Chapter 2: Uncovering your values — 23

Chapter 3: Noticing the messages you're receiving — 29

Chapter 4: Listening to the voices in your head — 37

Chapter 5: What assumptions are you making? — 45

Chapter 6: Living as if you value yourself — 51

Chapter 7: Getting rid of your Gremlins — 59

Chapter 8: Blibbles — 65

Chapter 9: Why are other people so weird? — 69

Chapter 10: I'm OK, you're OK — 75

Chapter 11: Daring to dream — 81

Chapter 12: Colouring in your future — 87

About the author

About the author

Described by clients as 'fun, fabulous and inspirational', Cathy's mission is to enable as many people as possible to realise their potential and be truly themselves at all times. Her philosophy is:

'Why live your life in a shade of grey, when you could show the world your true colours?'

Cathy spent 25 years in the Civil Service before escaping to set up her business, Colour In Your Thinking. She now uses her extensive experience in personal development, coaching and change management to work with students, mums and small business owners, and takes enormous delight in supporting her clients as they work towards achieving their goals.

This book came about as a result of seeing her (now adult) children and their friends go through the UK school and university system, and realising that there was little or no support in place for young people struggling to carve out their own place in the world. Cathy believes that, if you can come to know, love and accept yourself in your late teens/early twenties, then you're in the best place possible to realise your potential and plan for a successful future on your own terms.

Cathy is enormously proud of her children, and lives happily in Cheltenham with her lovely husband and two very fat cats.

Introduction

Introduction

You've decided to invest in your own future happiness and well-being – what could be more worthy of your time and money?

Life as a student can be bewildering. You're in a new environment, with new people and new opportunities available to you. Lots of people think that university is like school, except that you get away from your parents, you can call the teachers by their first names and every night is party night.

It doesn't take long to realise that it's not like that at all and you've actually entered a whole new world. You're away from all of your support networks. You're expected to think and behave like an adult, perhaps for the first time in your life. Everything familiar has gone and you're expected to throw yourself in, hit the ground running and embrace this new life from day one.

It's no surprise that so many people find this transition traumatic, and that universities spend a lot of time and money on trying to help their new intakes to adjust.

One of the things that lots of new students (and some not-so-new students) find disconcerting is being expected to make their own decisions. This is especially true of those who come from a home environment where they have either not needed or not been allowed to make their own decisions. Even if you've had a fairly liberal upbringing and feel that you've been taking responsibility for your own decisions for some time, university is still a whole different ball game.

Whereas before you may have had some money to spend on yourself from a part-time job or an allowance, now you have to learn to budget and pay for food, accommodation, travel, entertainment, study aids and all sorts of other things. How do you decide what to spend it on?

Also, whereas before you probably had a homework and revision schedule, with teachers and/or parents keeping an eye on your progress, now suddenly it's entirely up to you how much work you do and when – and there are so many other, possibly more enticing, things that you could be doing.

Then there is the way people treat you. While you're living at home and going to school, people still treat you like a child. Despite their best efforts, your parents can't help it (every time they look at you they're still seeing you in nappies, after all) and neither can your teachers. You'll probably have spent the last couple of years at home desperate to be free of it all and aching to be treated like an adult.

But then you come to university and everything changes.

Introduction

There's no parents' evening – your progress is a matter for discussion between you and your tutors. No one is going to ask for your parents' opinion or permission on anything any more, because you're an adult. That may be difficult for your parents to understand, but that's their problem, not yours.

You now have sole responsibility for looking after yourself – from getting to the right place at the right time with everything you need, to eating regularly and vaguely healthily, to making sure you manage your money effectively.

No matter how well prepared you think you are, this can still come as a shock, especially when you're trying to make friends, wondering whether you've done the right thing by coming here at all, and trying to pretend you're not feeling homesick and missing your mum.

'Be careful what you wish for, because you might just get it' has never rung so true.

Learning to respond effectively to being suddenly treated like an adult is a vital part of the transition that you need to make, but for some reason most of us are left to figure it out for ourselves. We flounder through on a mixture of bravado and shyness, learning from our mistakes and generally giving ourselves all sorts of reasons to wake up in a cold sweat, remembering some awful comment we made to a senior tutor or a fellow student when we thought we were being clever but weren't.

I can remember that feeling so well, and I've watched my own kids and their friends go through it in recent years.

> *So I've written this book with three aims:*
> 1. To help you to get to know, love and accept your true self;
> 2. To help you to manage the transition from child to adult as quickly and as gracefully as possible; and
> 3. To help you to decide on and plan for a happy and fulfilling future that suits the real you.

Are you ready to start taking active steps towards a more positive, confident future? Then let's get started!

Cathy

Chapter 1
This is me...
I think?

Chapter 1: This is me... I think?

Do you know who you are? If you do, do you like and accept who you are? Many of us spend our lives either not knowing who we really are, or pretending to be someone that we're not because we fear that no one would like us if they really knew us.

I believe that to be a terrible waste of potential and mental energy that could be better spent on realising that potential. Everyone has potential: often far more than they have the courage to admit to themselves, let alone to anyone else.

This is as true of you as it is of anyone else.

Everyone has the right to be themselves and live the life they choose to live, provided that they're not causing harm to others.

That, too, is as true of you as it is of anyone else.

One of my favourite quotes is by Marianne Williamson, from her book *A Return to Love*. She writes:

> "Our deepest fear is not that we are inadequate. Our deepest fear is that we are powerful beyond measure. It is our light, not our darkness that most frightens us. We ask ourselves, Who am I to be brilliant, gorgeous, talented, fabulous? Actually, who are you not to be? You are a child of God. Your playing small does not serve the world. There is nothing enlightened about shrinking so that other people won't feel insecure around you. We are all meant to shine, as children do. We were born to make manifest the glory of God that is within us. It's not just in some of us; it's in everyone. And as we let our own light shine, we unconsciously give other people permission to do the same. As we are liberated from our own fear, our presence automatically liberates others".

You are in a perfect position to start to let your own light shine (if you haven't already), and this book is here to help you do just that. So let's start by looking at who you really are, and how you feel about yourself.

Exercise

Use the following note pages to describe yourself. Unless you choose to share it, you are the only person who will ever read this, so be honest with yourself. Write about who you are, where you've come from and what you want out of life. Write about your hopes and fears and your secret dreams. Write about the things that wake you up in the night, and the things that make you feel warm and secure. Write about what makes you tick, your loves, likes and dislikes, the parts of you that you celebrate and the parts of you that make you despair. If this feels like a daunting task, try starting by describing a memory from your childhood and see what thoughts it leads you into. It doesn't matter how long you take or how many pages you cover, as long as you feel that you've done yourself justice when you've finished.

Chapter 1: This is me... I think?

Who am I?

Colour In Your Future... **FINDING THE REAL YOU**

Chapter 1: This is me... I think?

What worries you the most right now?

What makes you truly happy?

Chapter 1: This is me... I think?

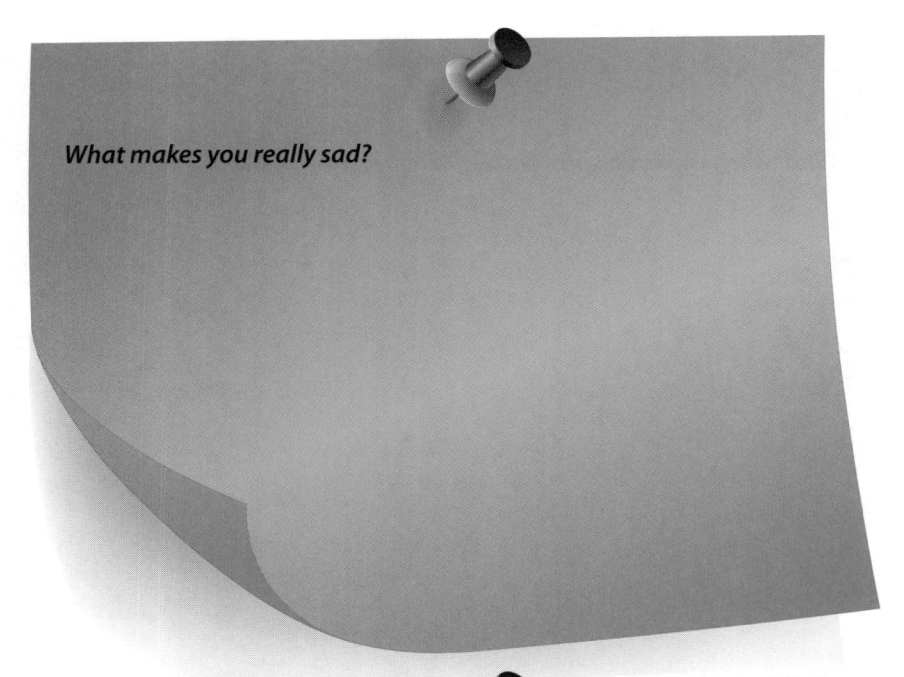

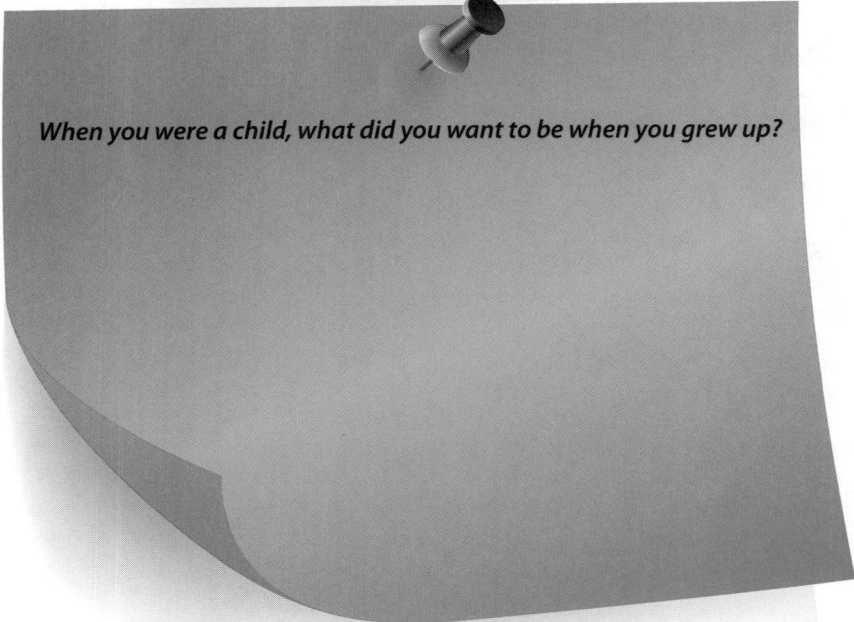

What makes you really sad?

When you were a child, what did you want to be when you grew up?

Colour In Your Future... **FINDING THE REAL YOU**

Chapter 1: This is me... I think?

What things have you promised yourself you would never do?

Who are your heroes?

Chapter 1: This is me... I think?

Put this book away for a while and go and do something completely different. I suggest you take a break of at least a couple of hours – coming back to it the next day would be even better. Your mind needs time to marinate!

Come back and read over what you've written. Notice what happens as you read, and write down the answers to the questions below.

What emotions do you feel?

What memories are triggered?

Colour In Your Future... **FINDING THE REAL YOU**

Chapter 1: This is me... I think?

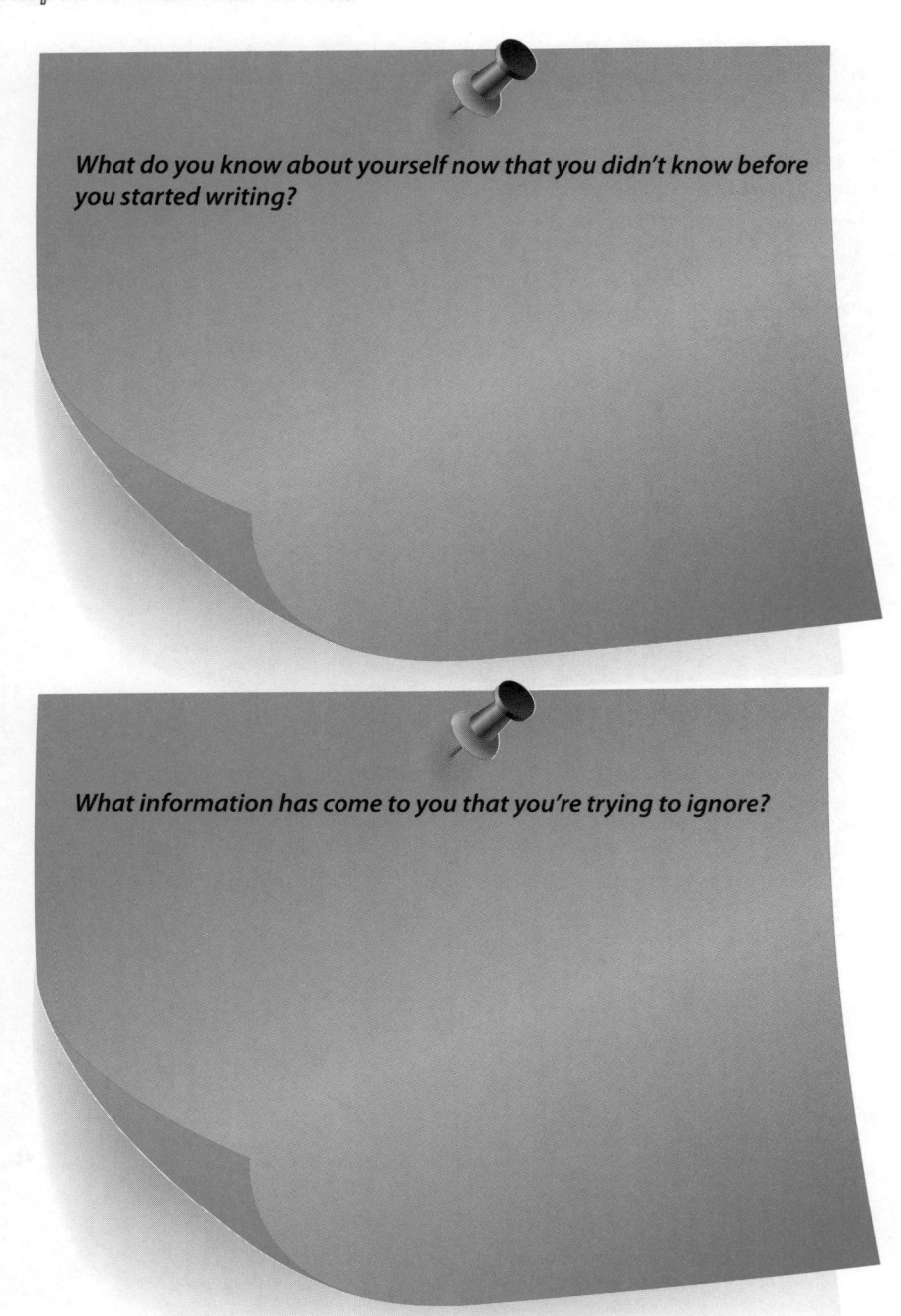

What do you know about yourself now that you didn't know before you started writing?

What information has come to you that you're trying to ignore?

Chapter 1: This is me... I think?

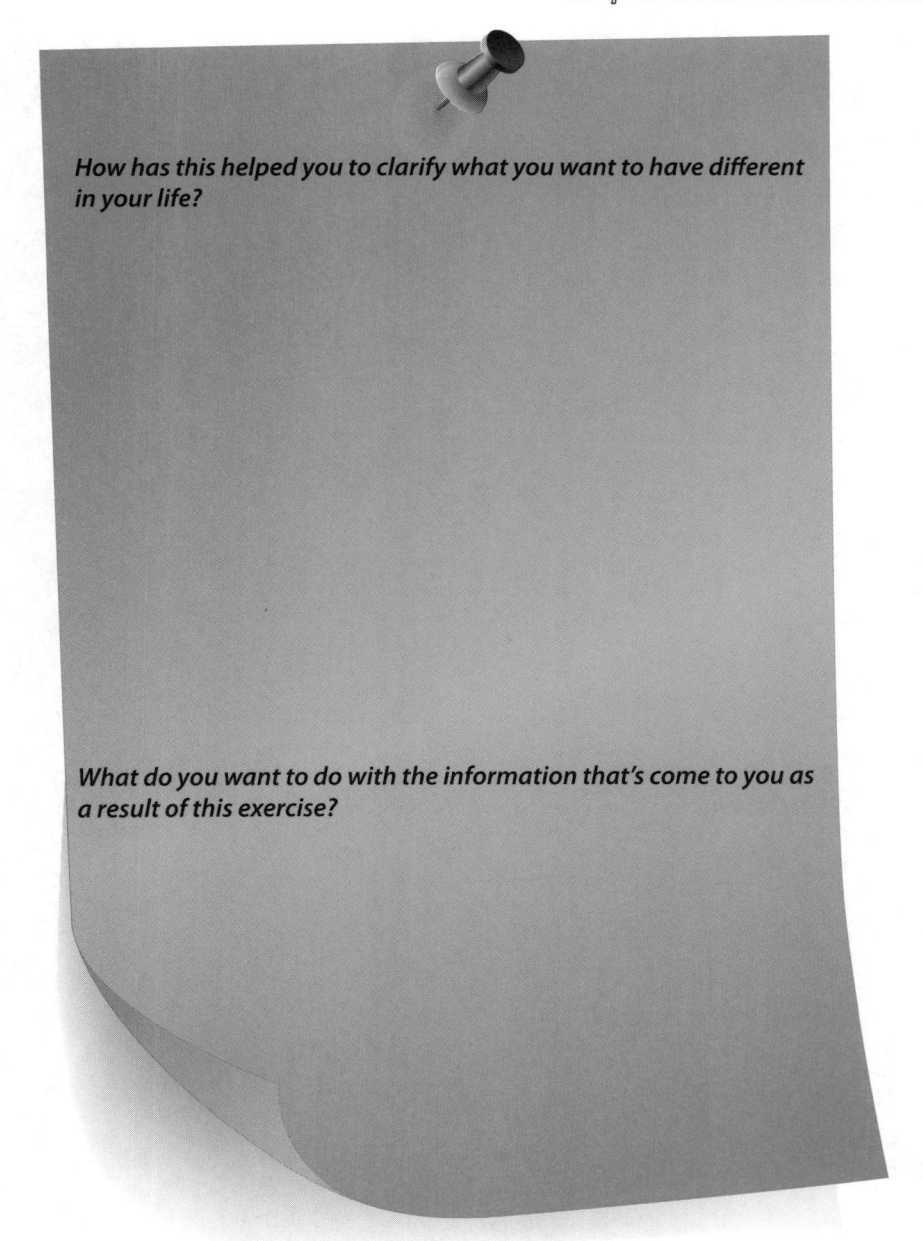

How has this helped you to clarify what you want to have different in your life?

What do you want to do with the information that's come to you as a result of this exercise?

Keep this exercise in the back of your mind as you work through the rest of the book – you'll find the results really useful.

Chapter 2
Uncovering your values

Chapter 2: Uncovering your values

Do you know what your values are? Many of us have an undefined idea of what is important to us, and we always know when someone says or does something that seems so wrong as to be offensive to us. Often we can be mystified by the fact that other people don't seem to agree with a belief or an opinion of ours – how can they not? Surely everyone knows that this is just the way things are?

Even with our nearest and dearest we can sometimes feel as if we're on different wavelengths, when they or we seem to have the 'wrong' opinions about what's truly important in life.

Do you recognise any of these situations?

> You and a friend have repeated arguments over whether or not fox hunting should be banned. Things have begun to get so heated that you're beginning to wonder whether you can continue to be friends.
>
> Every time you have an essay to finish or some reading that has to be done, your partner or your friends want you to come out and party with them instead. If you don't go they make you feel bad about letting them down, and if you do go, you spend the whole time angry and upset because you'd rather be working.
>
> Your parents are convinced that they know what's best for you and have spent years insisting that you should study what they want you to study. Now you're on a course doing what they want, but you hate it and would rather be doing something else that reflects what you really want. Whenever you try to talk to them about it, they get upset or angry and remind you of what they've given up for you.

These are all examples of the clash of different values and what can happen when we're not aware of what is going on. In each of these three examples, each party firmly believes that they are right and the other person is wrong. Indeed, so strongly do they believe that they are right, that they will expend a vast amount of energy trying to convince the other person of that fact.

This can go one of two ways:
1. Either the two parties find themselves trapped in an unending cycle of disagreement, which starts to colour the rest of the relationship and can lead to them developing an increasingly negative view of each other; or
2. One of the parties will become dominant, and the other party will attempt to subdue or adapt their own values so that they fit in. People do this for a number of reasons. For example, if you are lacking in self-confidence, it can be easy to become convinced that the other person is right and you are wrong (particularly if that's what you are being told). Or it may be that you prefer to avoid conflict – the easiest way is to go along with what someone else wants.

Neither of these situations is ideal, and both can be avoided once we become aware of our values, and realise that each of us has our own, unique set of values that colour our view of the world. You can think of values as the 'rules' that we live by, if that makes it easier. We've each constructed our own set of rules based on what's happened to us in our lives, and tension and misunderstanding arise when my rules and your rules clash.

It is perfectly possible to live a life that is not in tune with your values, but it comes at a cost. Over time it will lead to a deep sense of frustration and unhappiness, a feeling that we have betrayed ourselves or sold out. It is most definitely not the way to live if you want to show the world your true colours.

This exercise is designed to help you to start to identify at least some of your own personal values.

Exercise
Write down the names of the three people that you admire the most. They don't need to be people you know, so you could choose famous people or even fictional characters.

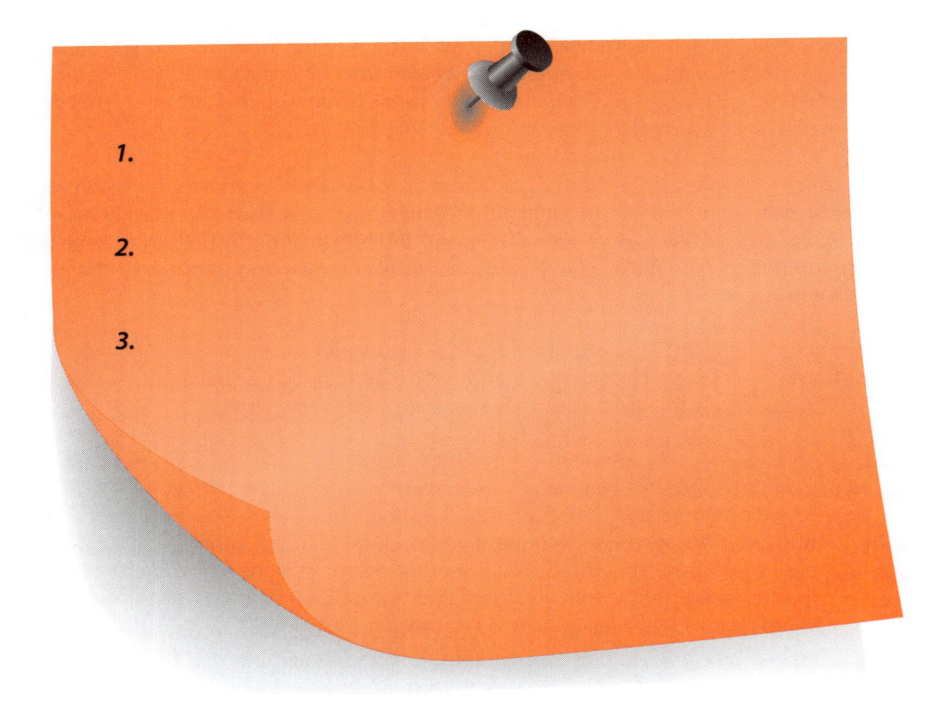

1.

2.

3.

Chapter 2: Uncovering your values

Now make a note of the particular qualities and characteristics that each of them has which makes them so admirable or inspiring in your eyes. Don't censor yourself by discounting qualities or characteristics that you think somehow are not worthy of inclusion.

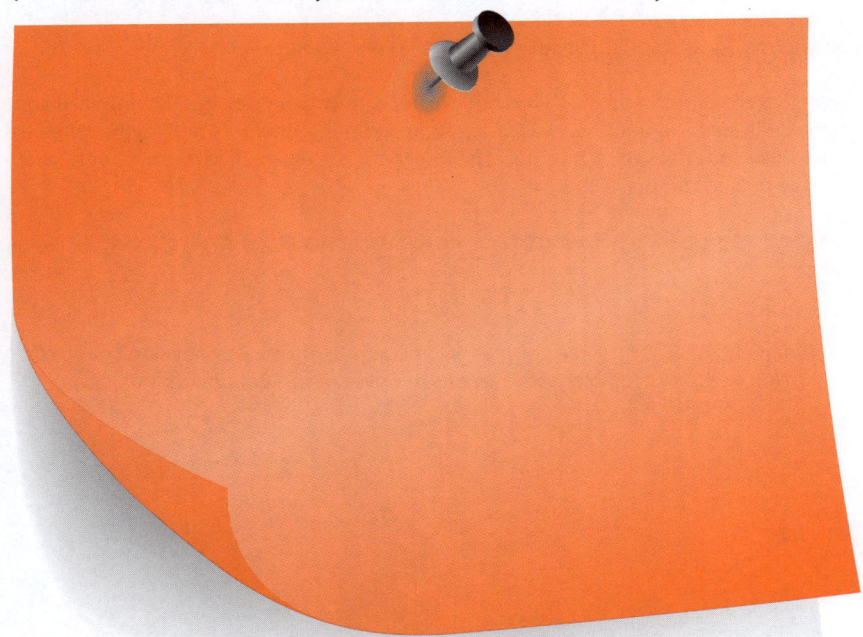

Now see if you can make any groupings of words. For example, does the same word crop up more than once, or have you used different words to mean roughly the same thing? See what groupings you can make, and decide on one word that sums up the content of each group, for example:

1. honesty – truthful, straightforward, candid, trustworthy
2. bravery – courage, courageous, stands up for people, likes a challenge
3. humour – likes to have fun, bubbly character, makes me laugh.

These headline words are a good indicator of what your values are. You won't have created an exhaustive list, but you'll have made a good start.

Write each of your values on a separate piece of paper – sticky notes are ideal for this purpose.

Now arrange those sheets of paper so that your values are set out in order of importance for you. This can be really difficult, so take your time and remember that there is no right or wrong answer. What you may find is that it's quite easy to identify the ones that are critically important to you, and much more difficult with the rest. Don't worry about it!

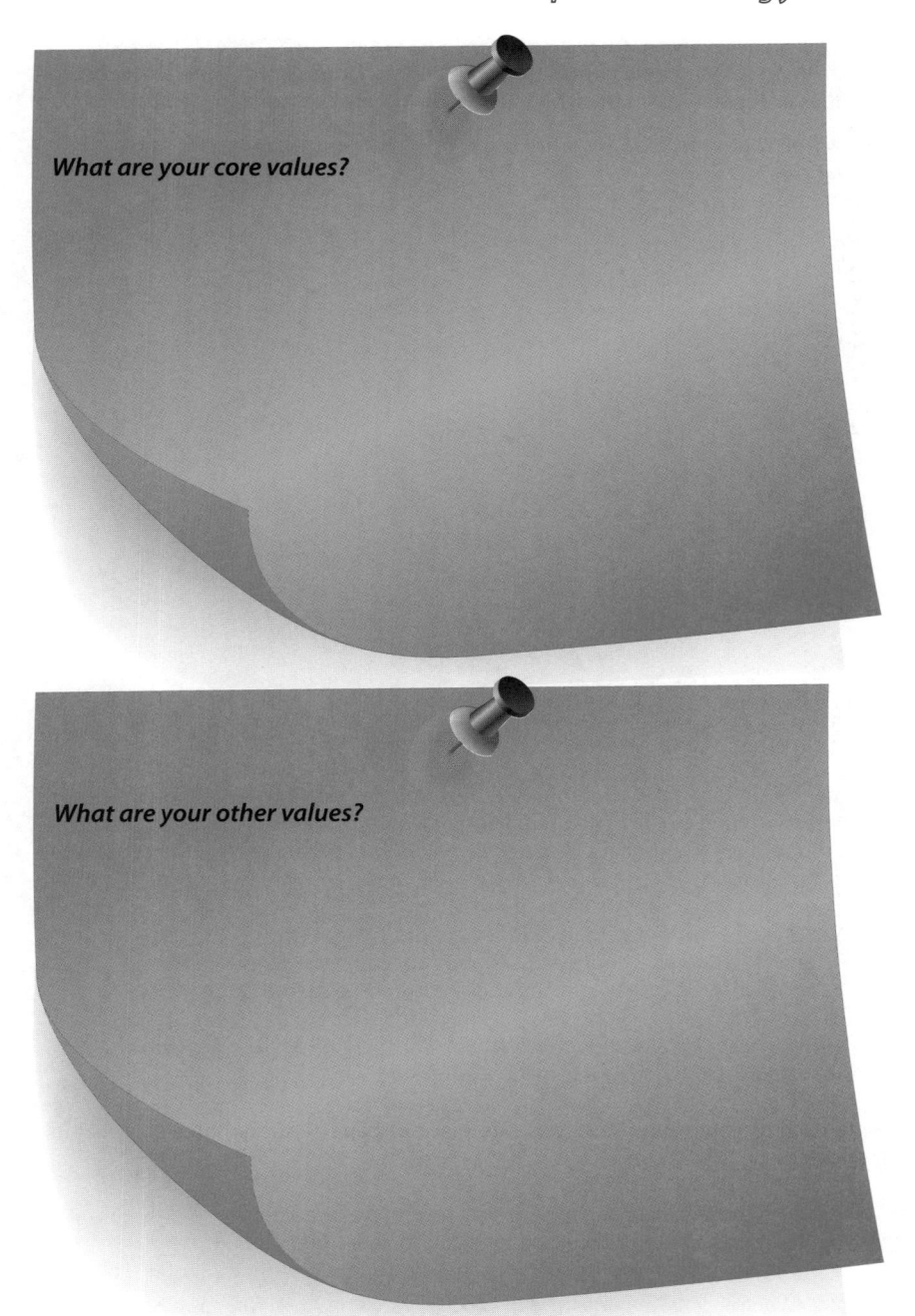

Chapter 2: Uncovering your values

What are your core values?

What are your other values?

Colour In Your Future... **FINDING THE REAL YOU**

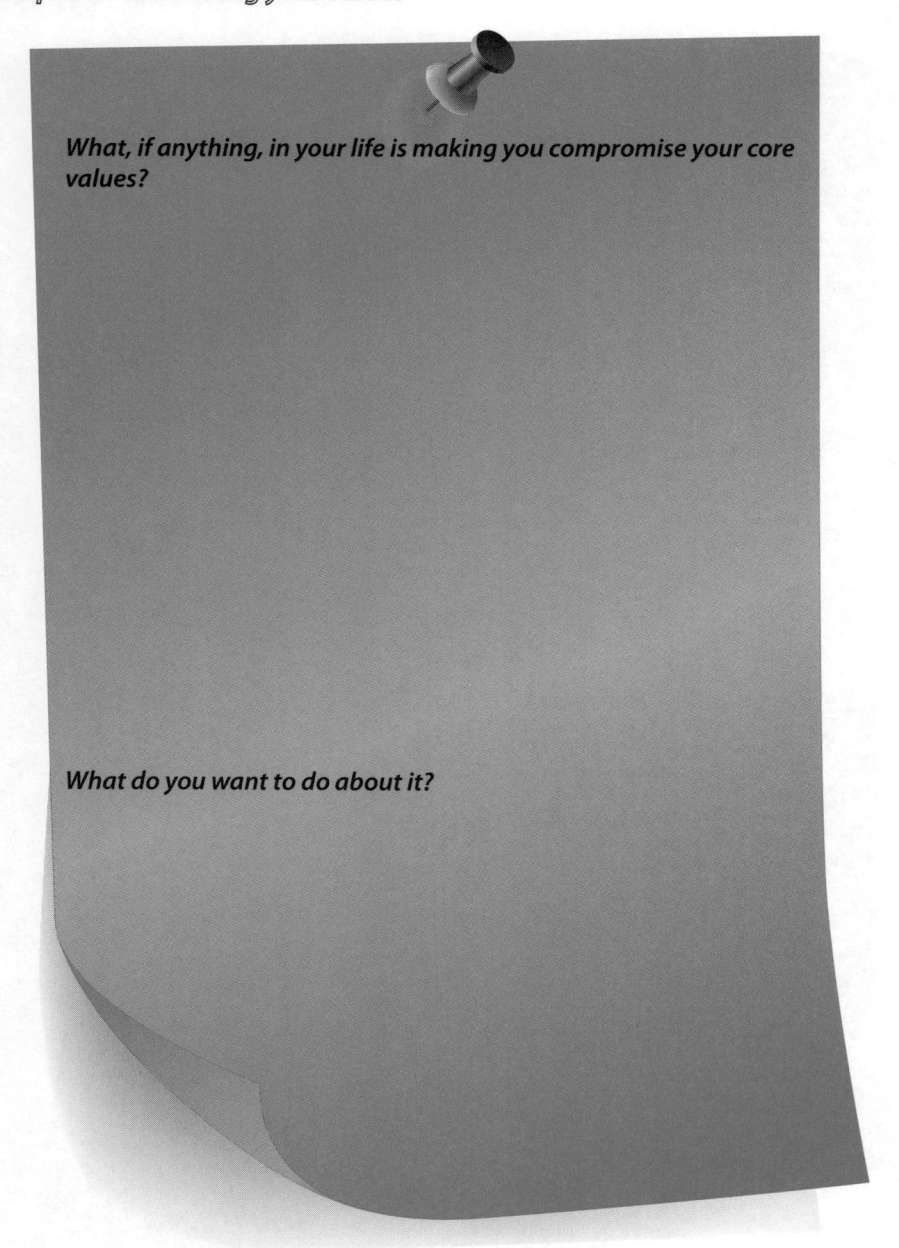

Chapter 2: Uncovering your values

What, if anything, in your life is making you compromise your core values?

What do you want to do about it?

What you've done is identify the values that you simply won't compromise – let's call them your core values – and the ones where you'll allow some room for manoeuvre.

Chapter 3
Noticing the messages you're receiving

Chapter 3: Noticing the messages you're receiving

Every day we are bombarded with messages from the world around us about who we are and who other people think we should be.

These messages come at us from all directions: many adverts, for example, seem to be designed to make us feel bad about ourselves, so that we'll spend money on their product in the hope it will make us feel better because somehow we've become more acceptable.

Some of us find it easier to ignore those messages than others, and some of us are better at filtering out the ones that we don't want to hear than others. What is interesting is what constitutes your personal criteria for 'I don't want to hear it' messages.

- Are you someone who doesn't want to hear anything that could possibly be criticism, even if it might actually be helpful to you?
- Are you someone who can't bear praise or compliments, or refuses to believe that they could be true?
- Do you even know what you're filtering out? Don't worry if you don't. Your filtering is going on at the subconscious level, so unless you look out for it, it's no surprise that you don't know what's going on.

As well as all this filtering, we're also very good at assuming that we know what people think of us, and we use those assumptions to guide our behaviour rather than looking for the evidence of what they tell us. There is more about assumptions in Chapter 5; for now, it's enough to say that until we actually start taking note of what people say and what they do (rather than what we think they might say and do), it's dangerous to assume that we know anything about what they're thinking.

This exercise is designed to help you to do three things:
1. To take note of all the messages about you that are coming your way;
2. To discover which ones you're filtering out, and why; and
3. To consciously choose some positive filters to use from now on.

So if you're ready, let's start.

Exercise

For the next week, every time one of the following things happens, make a note of it in the following blank pages.

Someone makes a comment to you about you: it could be about how you look, something you've done, their perception of how you are, a thank you, anything at all that reveals how they feel about you in that moment. Don't forget to include comments in writing from emails or letters – it doesn't have to be face-to-face stuff.

Chapter 3: Noticing the messages you're receiving

- You overhear a comment that you think is about you (not that I'm suggesting eavesdropping, but it can happen from time to time by accident!).
- A third party passes on to you a comment that somebody else made about you.
- You come across an advertisement or something in the media that seems to you to be addressing you or people like you.

Don't beat yourself up if you can't catch every last one, but do remain attentive and focus on the messages you're receiving. Once you've started, you'll find it gets easier as time goes on.

Be rigorous and reject your filters. Don't allow yourself to discount anything.

Messages

Chapter 3: Noticing the messages you're receiving

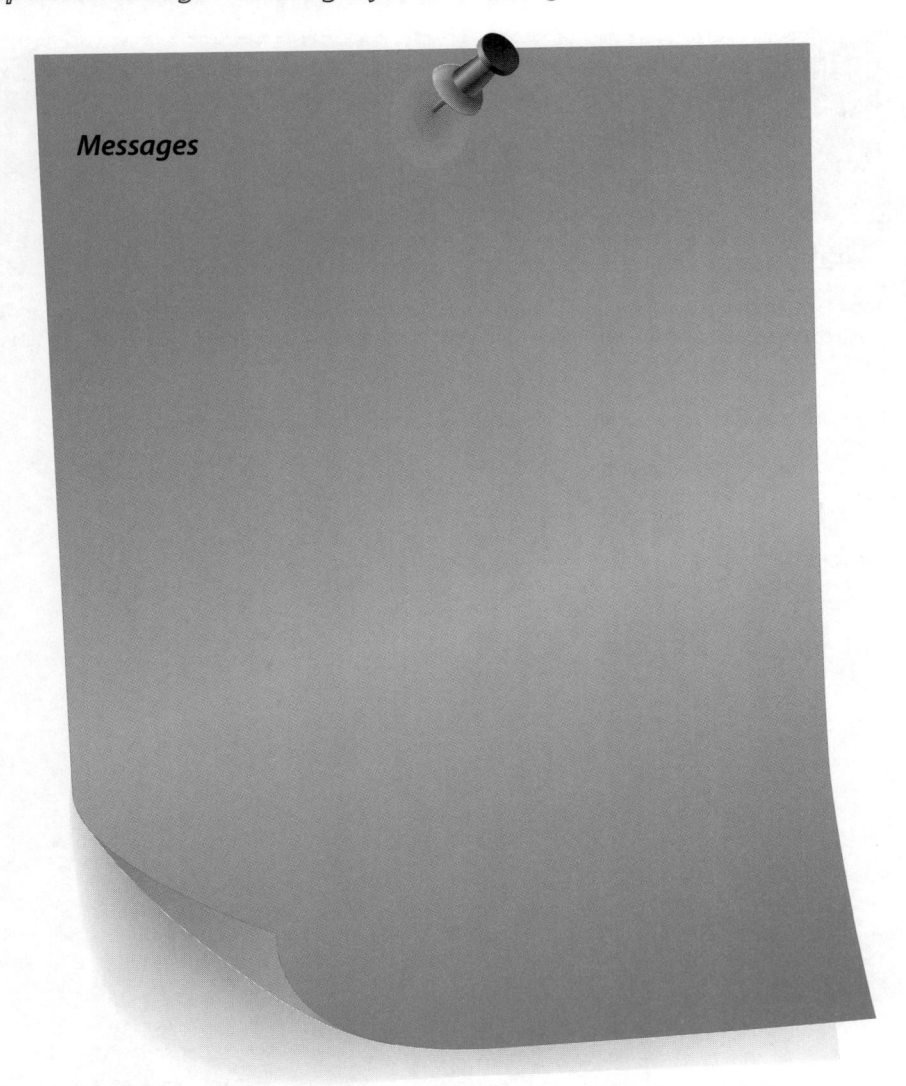

Messages

At the end of the week, you are likely to have become aware of at least some of your filters, because you'll have spotted the messages that you wanted to ignore.

Go back through all of the messages you've noted down, and highlight the positive ones, even if they make you feel uncomfortable.

Now go back through the complete list, and *mark in a different colour the ones that normally you would have discounted.*

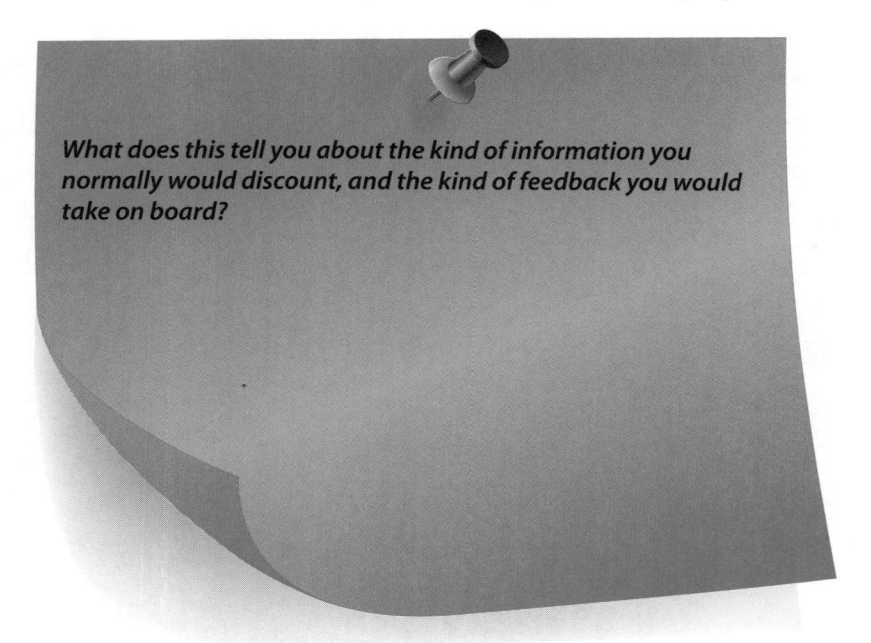

Chapter 3: Noticing the messages you're receiving

What does this tell you about the kind of information you normally would discount, and the kind of feedback you would take on board?

Look again at the messages that you reject and answer the following questions.

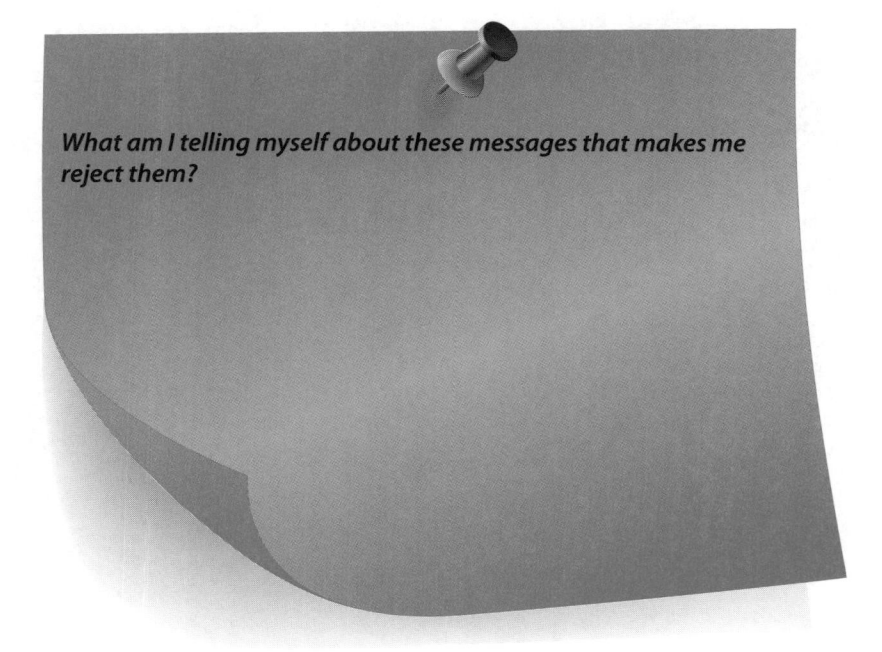

What am I telling myself about these messages that makes me reject them?

Colour In Your Future... **FINDING THE REAL YOU**

Chapter 3: Noticing the messages you're receiving

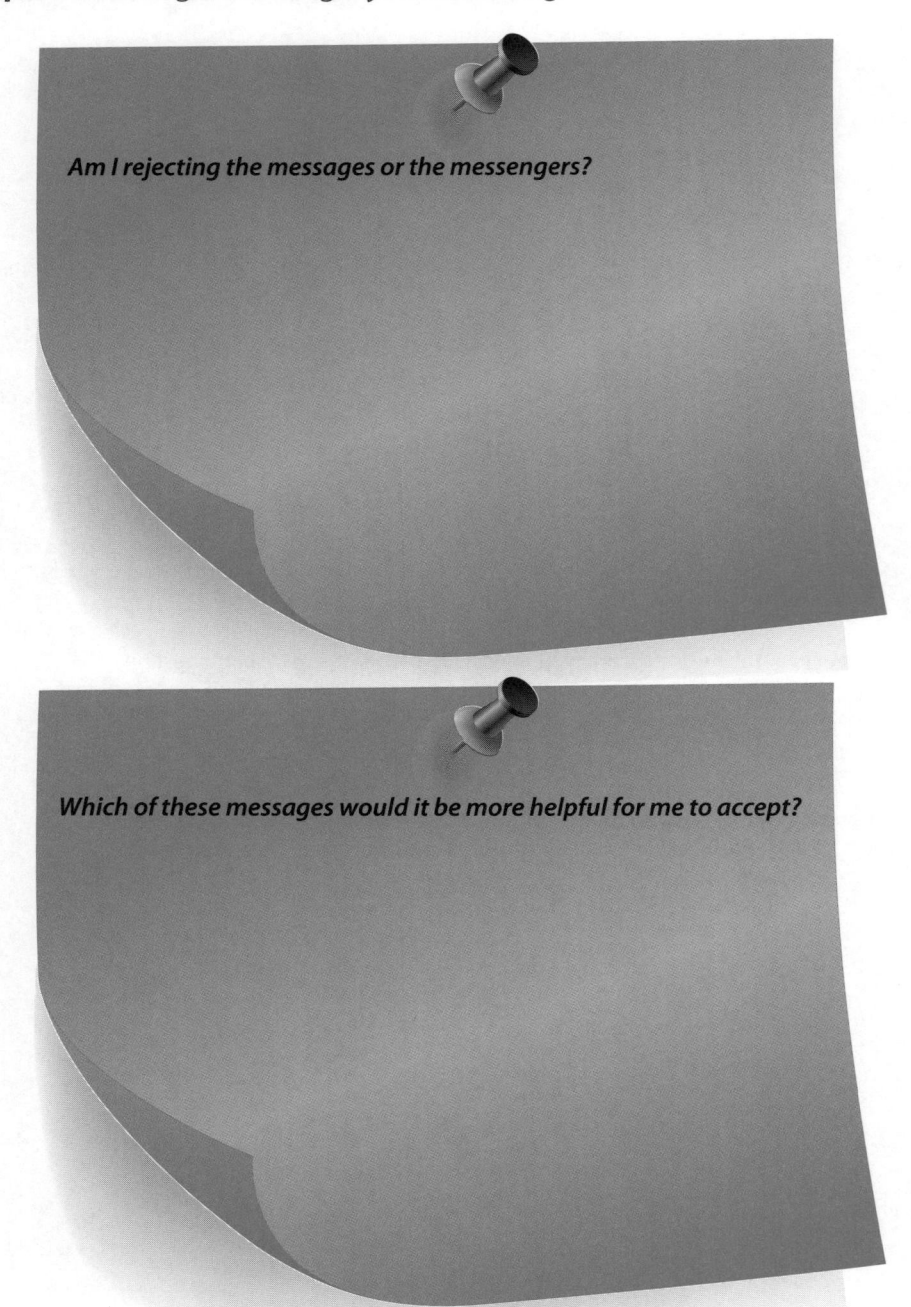

Am I rejecting the messages or the messengers?

Which of these messages would it be more helpful for me to accept?

Chapter 3: Noticing the messages you're receiving

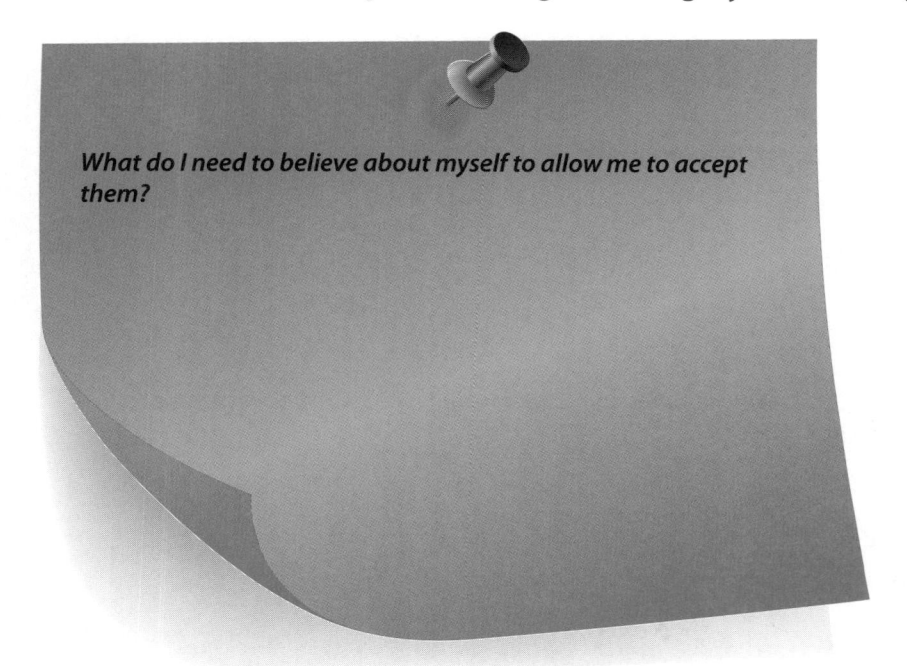

What do I need to believe about myself to allow me to accept them?

Now look at the messages that you accept and ask yourself the following questions.

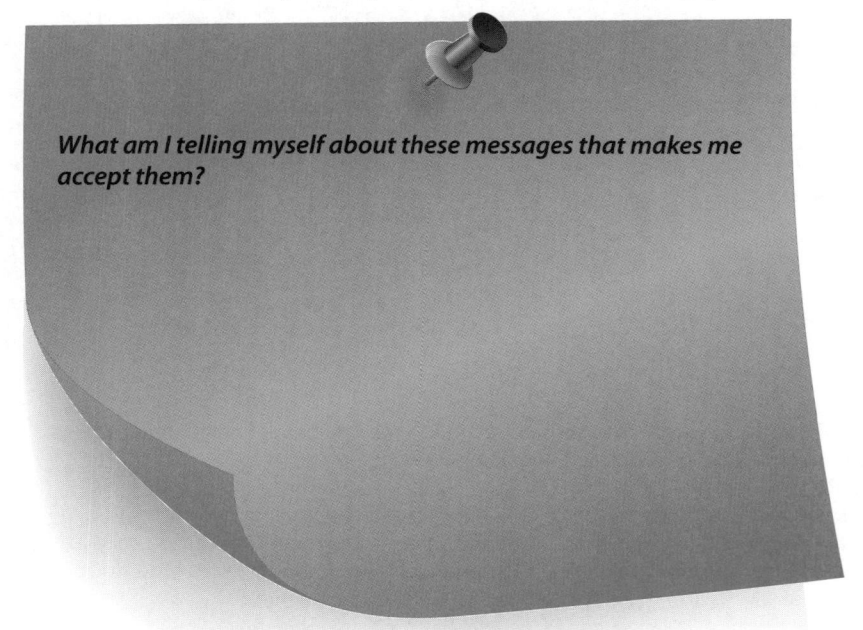

What am I telling myself about these messages that makes me accept them?

Colour In Your Future... **FINDING THE REAL YOU**

Chapter 3: Noticing the messages you're receiving

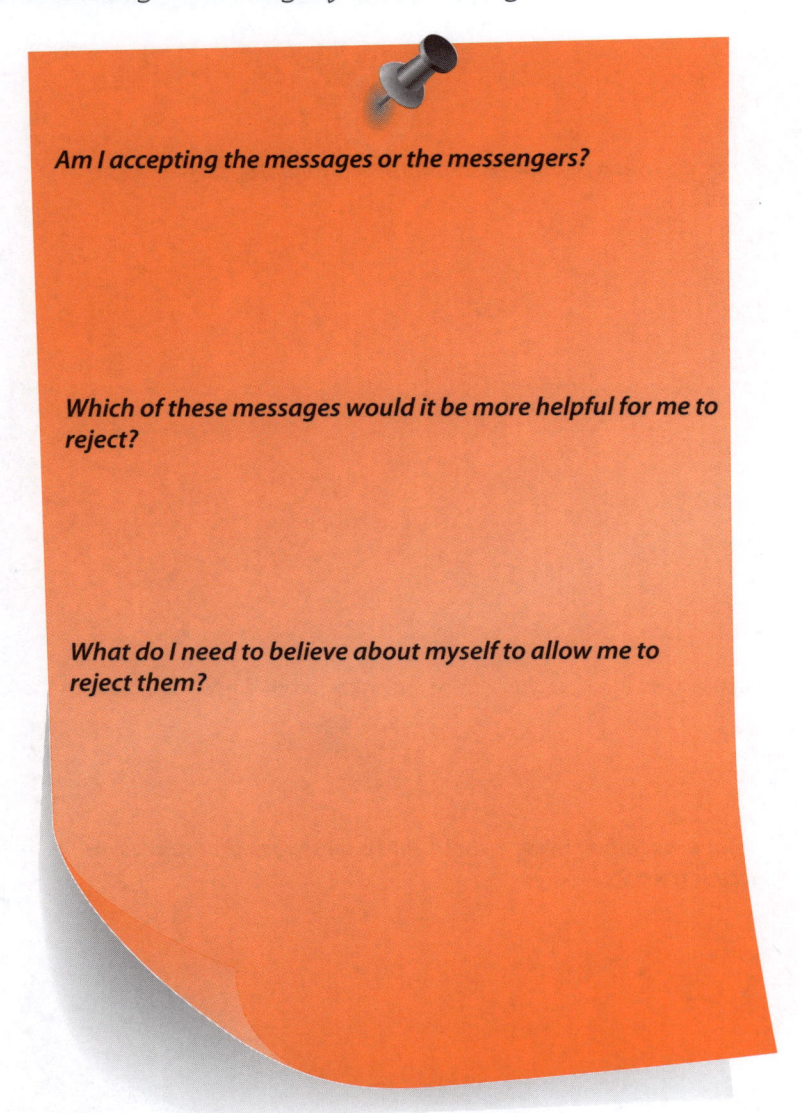

Am I accepting the messages or the messengers?

Which of these messages would it be more helpful for me to reject?

What do I need to believe about myself to allow me to reject them?

Armed with the answers to those questions, you may be in a position already to choose some new filters for yourself. If not, don't worry.

Put this exercise to the back of your mind and get on with your normal routine. Your mind is a wonderful thing and it will continue to chew this over until it feels ready to let you know what your new filters are. This time it will be your choice whether to accept your filters, or whether to reject them.

Chapter 4
Listening to the voices in your head

Chapter 4: Listening to the voices in your head

Ah, the voices in your head. Don't worry, we've all got them! If you're currently having a conversation with yourself along the lines of 'What's she talking about? I don't hear voices!', well, who are you talking to?

What does your inner voice tell you about yourself, and how much attention do you pay to it? Are you even aware of it? We chunter away to ourselves all day, every day, recording our own 'director's commentary' on our lives. Sometimes we're aware of it happening and sometimes not.

Your inner voice has an incredibly powerful effect on you, whether you're aware of it or not. By learning to tune into it rather than ignoring it, or worse, trying to suppress it, you can harness it as a powerful tool to help build your self-confidence. Here's an example from my own experience.

Example
I was finding it really difficult to switch off at night, and found myself waking up at 4am with my head spinning with all the stuff I had to do, which led to getting up at silly o'clock to get work done and then fretting when I couldn't think clearly. After a couple of days I was in a bit of a state, and soon all I wanted to do was sit in a corner and cry. Instead of doing that, I took myself off to bed for some quiet time to think, drink tea and calm down.

I listened very hard to what was going on in my head and realised that my inner voice was chuntering away along these lines:

> "You've got to think about marketing and you need a PR strategy and there's that workshop you're running on Saturday and you need to be ready for that and have you contacted the people that are coming yet and you're nearly out of business cards and you need to hold a teleseminar and it's about time you recorded another podcast and when are you going to find somewhere for your workshops and if you held a seminar would anyone come and what kind of cupcakes are you going to make and... and... and..."

It's no wonder I couldn't sleep! Once I started to pay attention to what my inner voice was saying, I immediately realised that I was stressing myself out because I had fallen into one of my usual self-inflicted 'bear-traps': I had got so swept up with the excitement of new things that I'd stopped planning and prioritising, and now I couldn't see the wood for the trees.

So, instead of just letting the inner voice keep going and driving me mad, I decided to pay it some attention, and I wrote down all the things it was telling me I needed to do. This immediately helped me to feel calmer. It's like paying attention to a small child: if you ignore it, it just gets more and more persistent and insistent, tugging at your sleeve, getting louder, climbing all over you until you get completely exasperated with it. If you listen to what it's saying (provided that you're not in the middle of something critical) and acknowledge what it's trying to tell you, it will be happy and wander off to do something else, leaving you to concentrate on what you were doing.

Chapter 4: Listening to the voices in your head

So I acknowledged my inner voice, recognising that in this instance, it was trying to help me. Once I'd written down all the things it was reminding me about, I was able to prioritise them and recognise that actually only a very few needed my attention that week, so the rest could wait. Another huge weight off my shoulders, and a lessening of my stress.

Then, of course, I acknowledged that what I need is to draw up a plan and stick to it, rather than getting carried away with things and wanting to do it all now – and this from a woman who was renowned in her last job for chafing against the need to be tied down by plans!

So what is your inner voice telling you, and how helpful is it? This exercise is designed to help you work that out.

Exercise
Over the next couple of days, take time out to notice what your inner voice is saying to you and write it down in the following pages.

Don't censor it – nobody but you needs to know what it's saying.

Don't expect to be able to catch everything it says to you, but do put aside five minutes every now and again to tune into it. It often comes through more clearly when you're doing something that doesn't require you to think about what you're doing.

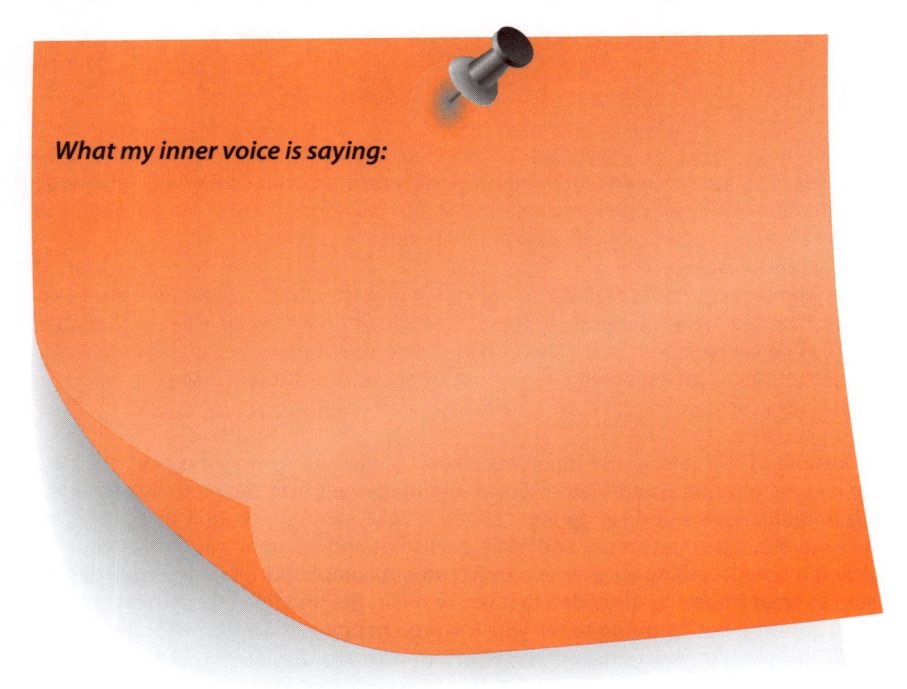

What my inner voice is saying:

Colour In Your Future... **FINDING THE REAL YOU**

Chapter 4: Listening to the voices in your head

Once you've captured a couple of days' worth, read through the things that your inner voice has said to you.

What strikes you about the messages that you're giving yourself?

Now highlight everything negative that you have told yourself about who/how/what you are.

Here are some examples:
- "I'll never get the hang of..."
- "... is too difficult for me"
- "I don't like..."
- "I could never do..."
- "I'm scared of..."
- "I'm not..."

Notice how many of these statements are made in absolute terms: for example, I am a failure, I can't do maths, I am stupid.

Now highlight, in a different colour, everything positive you have told yourself about who/how/what you are.

Again, notice how many of these statements are made in absolute terms: for example, I am good at what I do, I am pleased with myself, I am a success. Notice whether or not there is

Chapter 4: Listening to the voices in your head

a difference between the positive and negative statements in terms of how absolute they are.

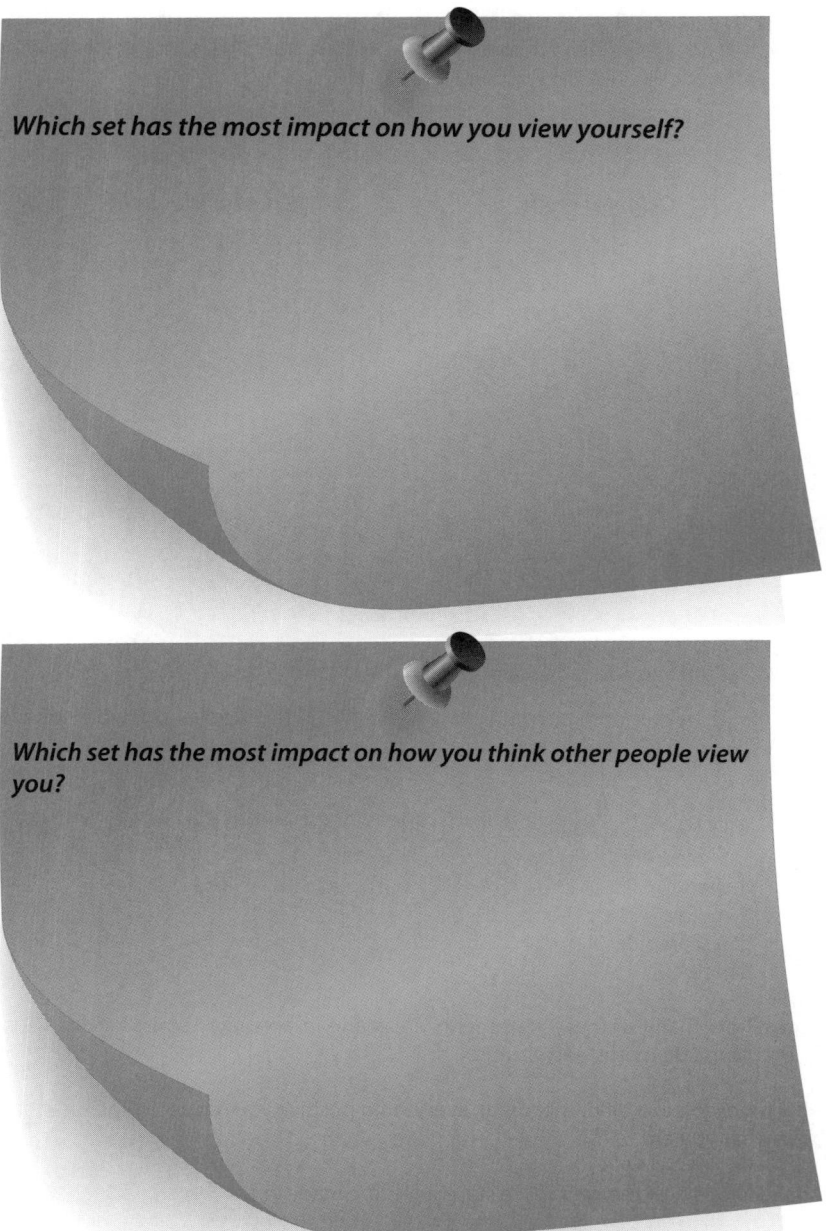

Which set has the most impact on how you view yourself?

Which set has the most impact on how you think other people view you?

Chapter 4: Listening to the voices in your head

Look again at your list of negative beliefs about yourself, particularly the ones that are absolute, and see if you can reword them in a way that makes them less absolute. The easiest way to do this is to replace the verb 'to be' with another verb, such as 'to feel'. For example, 'I am a failure' could become 'I feel like a failure'. See how many of your negative statements you can reword in this way.

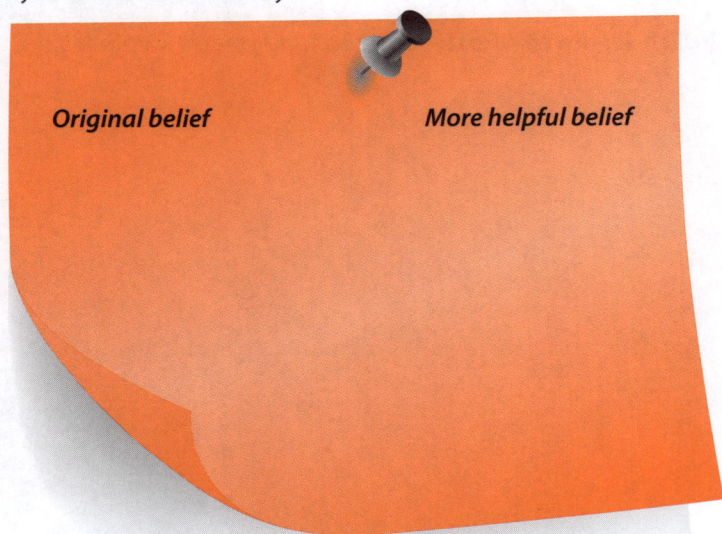

Original belief **More helpful belief**

Take some time now to reflect and answer the following questions:

What have you noticed about the messages you send yourself?

Chapter 4: Listening to the voices in your head

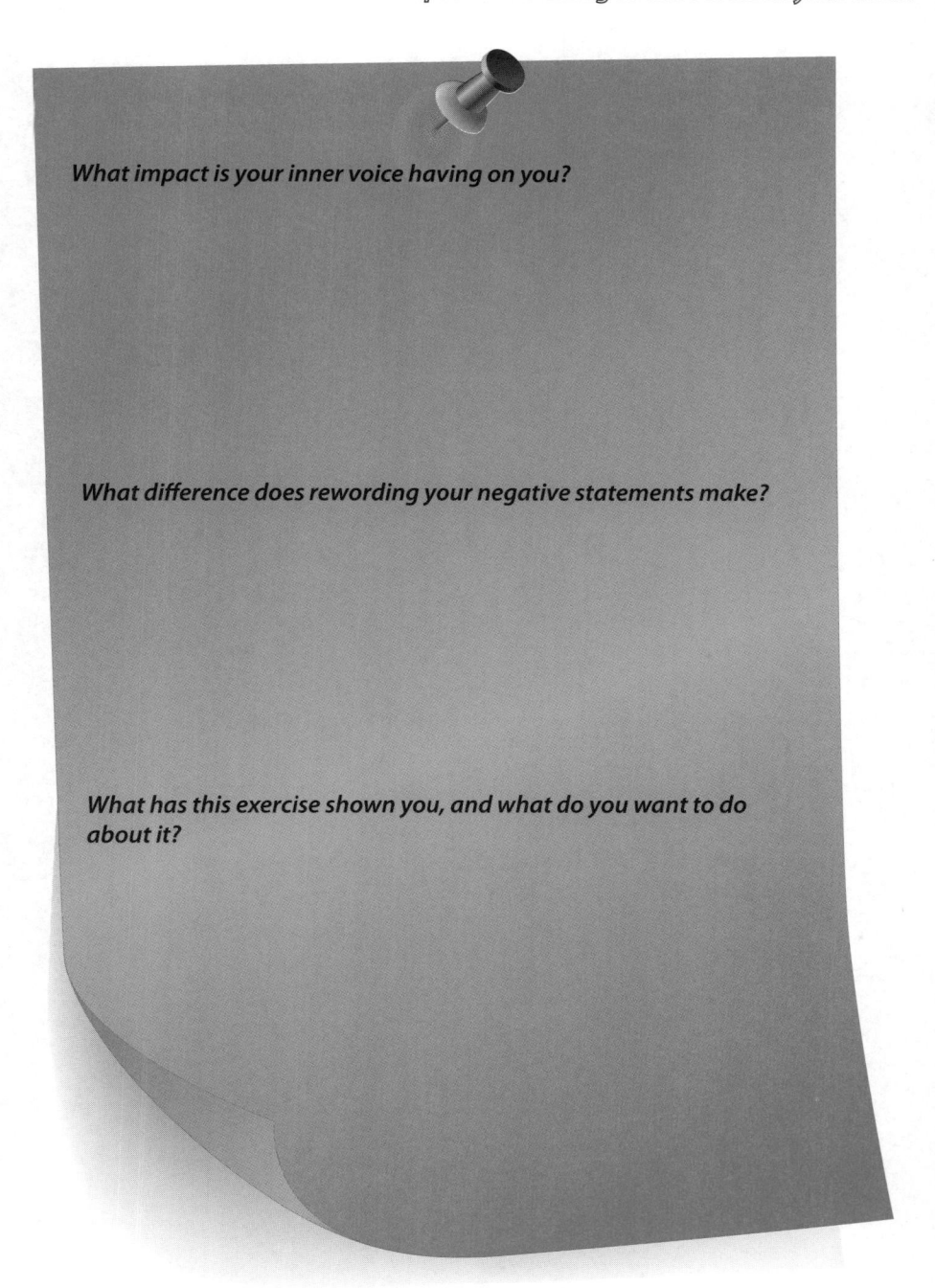

What impact is your inner voice having on you?

What difference does rewording your negative statements make?

What has this exercise shown you, and what do you want to do about it?

Chapter 5
What assumptions are you making?

Chapter 5: What assumptions are you making?

Uncovering the unhelpful assumptions that you're making about yourself and your life is the first step to being able to replace them with helpful assumptions, and doing that is a great way of increasing your self-confidence.

Everyone makes assumptions. It's a very useful thing to do because it stops our brains from exploding! Think about it: your brain is constantly taking in new information. It is being bombarded with sights, sounds, smells and goodness knows what else, and if it had to treat all of this information as brand new all the time, it wouldn't be able to function and you wouldn't be able to make sense of the world.

What your brain does is to use shortcuts to enable it to process the information that is coming in and to decide what to do with it. Assumptions are what it uses as its shortcuts. So, once you've encountered something once (or more, if it's complicated), the next time you encounter it, your brain will reach into its 'filing cabinet' and pull out the instructions on what to do. The first few times it might have to think about it a bit to remember which drawer to go to in which filing cabinet, but after a while it becomes automatic and neither you nor your brain needs to pay any attention to the process.

Most of the time that's fine – it's generally useful to assume that, if a car is racing towards you at 60mph, you need to get out of the way – but sometimes we hold on to assumptions that are unhelpful or outdated, and this is where we can make life difficult for ourselves.

Here's an example.

> Angela was badly bullied at school because she 'didn't fit in' with her peers: she liked classical music, read for pleasure and was a committed Christian, and that marked her out as a target. It was clear to her that other people thought that there was something wrong with the 'real her', and since there were so many of them and only one of her, that must be what everyone else thought as well. This resulted in her becoming even shyer than she already was, and finding it very difficult to make friends with people. This continued after school had ended, and still has an impact on her life, sapping her confidence and isolating her from the people around her. Now she is at university and finding it really difficult to make friends. Everyone around her seems to be really confident and having a good time and that makes things even worse. Not only does Angela feel as if she is the only one who isn't settling in, but she finds herself constantly worrying about how she is doing and comparing herself to the others on her course. Although she has left school and moved to a completely new part of the country, in lots of ways it feels to her as though nothing has changed, and nothing ever will.

Here are some of the unhelpful assumptions that Angela is making about herself and her life (you might have spotted more).

- The things I like to do aren't acceptable/normal.
- People won't like me if they get to know the real me.
- If I try to get to know people, I'll get bullied again.

Chapter 5: What assumptions are you making?

- Everyone else is doing better than I am.
- My life sucks, and it always will.

In order to start to turn things around, Angela first needs to notice the unhelpful assumptions that she is making, then replace them with more helpful assumptions, such as the following.

- It's up to me to decide what I enjoy doing.
- If I try to get to know other people, I could find some really good friends.
- Just because I was bullied once, it doesn't mean it's going to happen again.
- I don't know how anyone else is doing, and comparing myself to others isn't helpful anyway.
- Just because I'm not very happy now, it doesn't follow that I'm always going to feel this way.

What assumptions are you making about yourself and your life that are no longer valid or helpful? Perhaps they never were!

This exercise aims to bring to light assumptions that you might not have been aware of making, so that you can decide whether or not they are helpful to you.

Exercise
Look back at the 'Story of You' that you wrote back in Chapter 1. Read through it and highlight every assumption that you notice. If you find this difficult, and you have someone in your life that you trust implicitly and know will not be judgemental, you may want to ask them to read through it and spot the assumptions for you. Write down your assumptions on the following piece of notepaper.

My assumptions

Chapter 5: What assumptions are you making?

Now highlight the assumptions that are *unhelpful* to you.

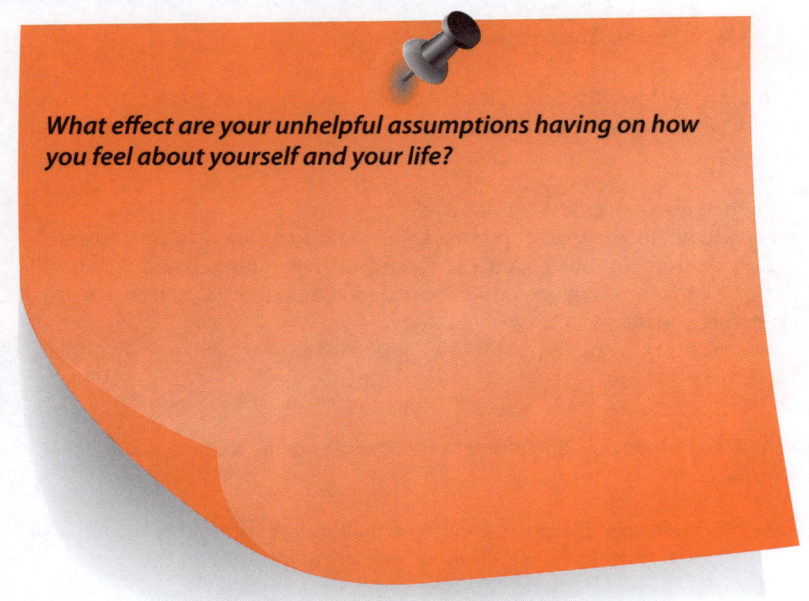

What effect are your unhelpful assumptions having on how you feel about yourself and your life?

Write down some new, more helpful assumptions to replace your old, unhelpful ones. The easiest way to do this is to take an unhelpful assumption and write the opposite. So, the assumption: 'There's no point in trying because I'll only fail' could become: 'If I try, I might succeed.'

My new assumptions

Chapter 5: What assumptions are you making?

What would you do differently if you lived your life with these new assumptions in place?

What new ideas and possibilities have come to you as a result of this exercise? Make sure to note them all down – this is a moment to be captured.

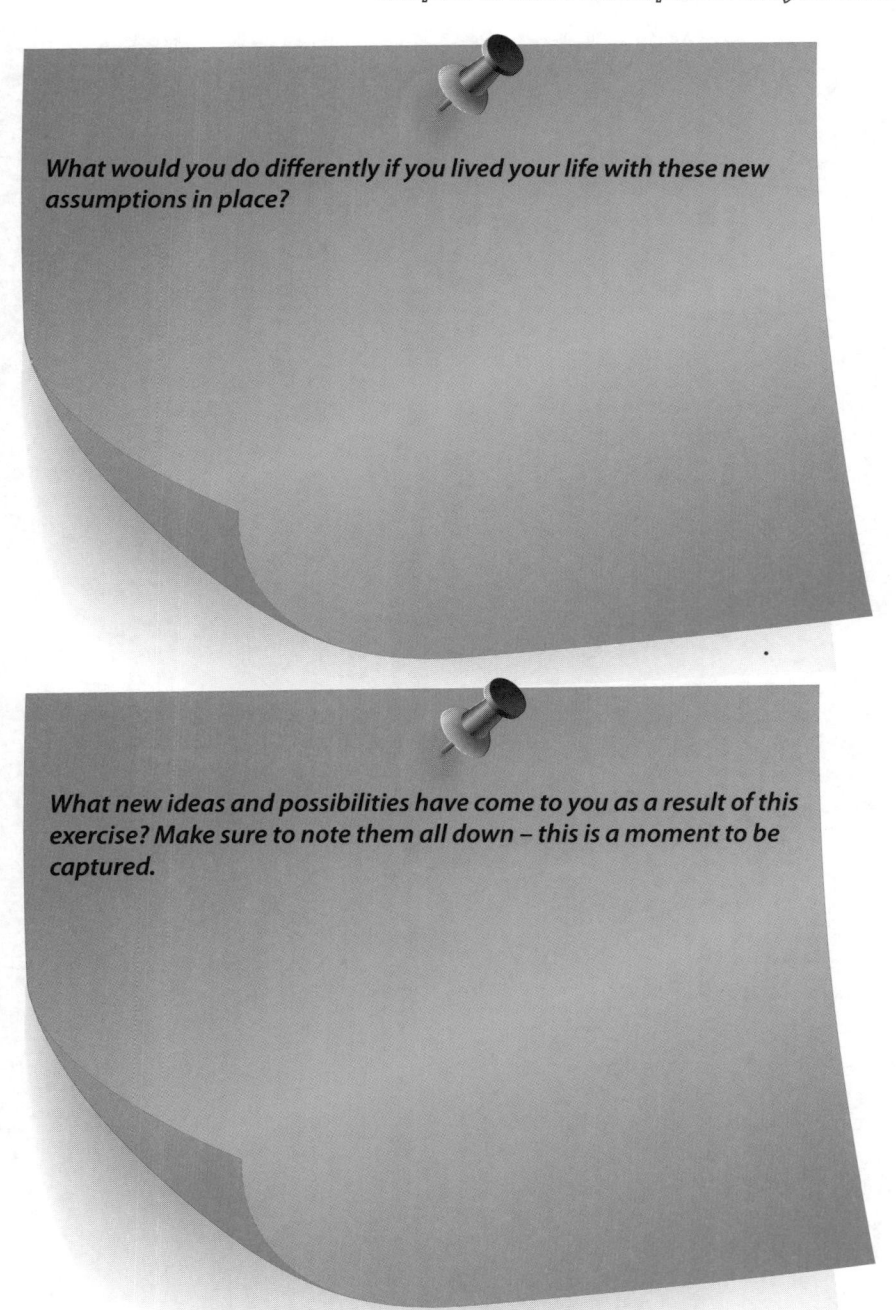

Chapter 6
Living as if you value yourself

Chapter 6: Living as if you value yourself

Do you live as if you value yourself, or are you treating yourself as if you were worthless? However well you may think you conceal it, the value you put on yourself is usually pretty clear to the rest of the world. We all know people who are considered to be 'full of themselves': what this expression really means is that the value that those individuals give to themselves is out of kilter with the value that other people place on them. Similarly, we've all seen people in certain situations and thought (maybe even said) 'You're worth more than that' or 'You're better than that'.

This exercise is designed to help you to take an objective look at yourself so that you can make a true assessment of your own worth. Whether you have been overvaluing or undervaluing yourself, wouldn't you rather be able to stand four-square and say, simply and easily, 'This is who I am and this is my rightful place?' When you learn to value yourself, this is exactly what happens – and the impact is incredible.

So, if you're sitting comfortably, let's begin.

Exercise
Think about someone you value deeply and for whom you want only the best. If you have a young cousin or sibling, that's a good way to go, but a beloved partner, parent or friend would be a good choice too.

Imagine you had complete control over how that person lived their life (this is why it's easier if you're thinking about a small child!). As we've said, you want only the best for them. To me, that means ensuring that they are happy, healthy, loved and secure. What does it mean to you?

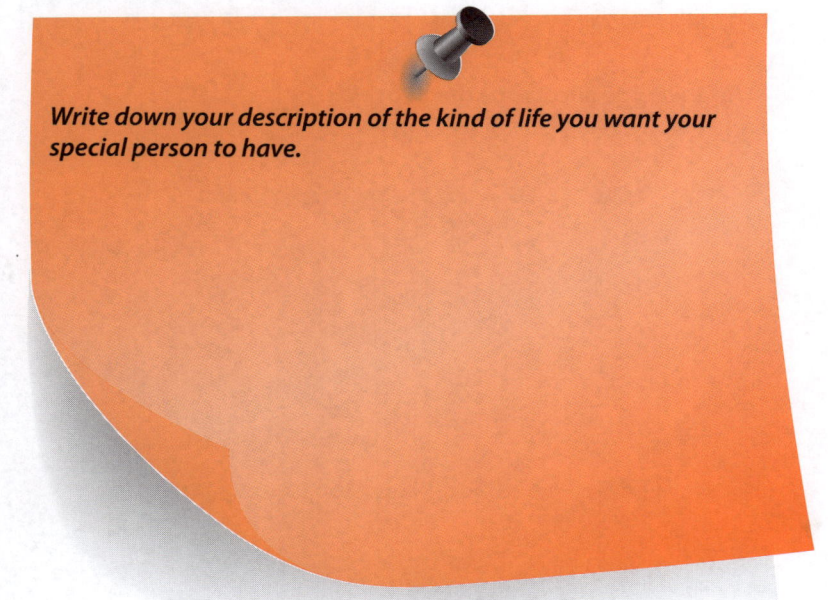

Write down your description of the kind of life you want your special person to have.

Chapter 6: Living as if you value yourself

Now note down all the things you would do to ensure that your special person got to live that kind of life. You may find the following questions helpful, but do bear in mind that it isn't an exhaustive list.

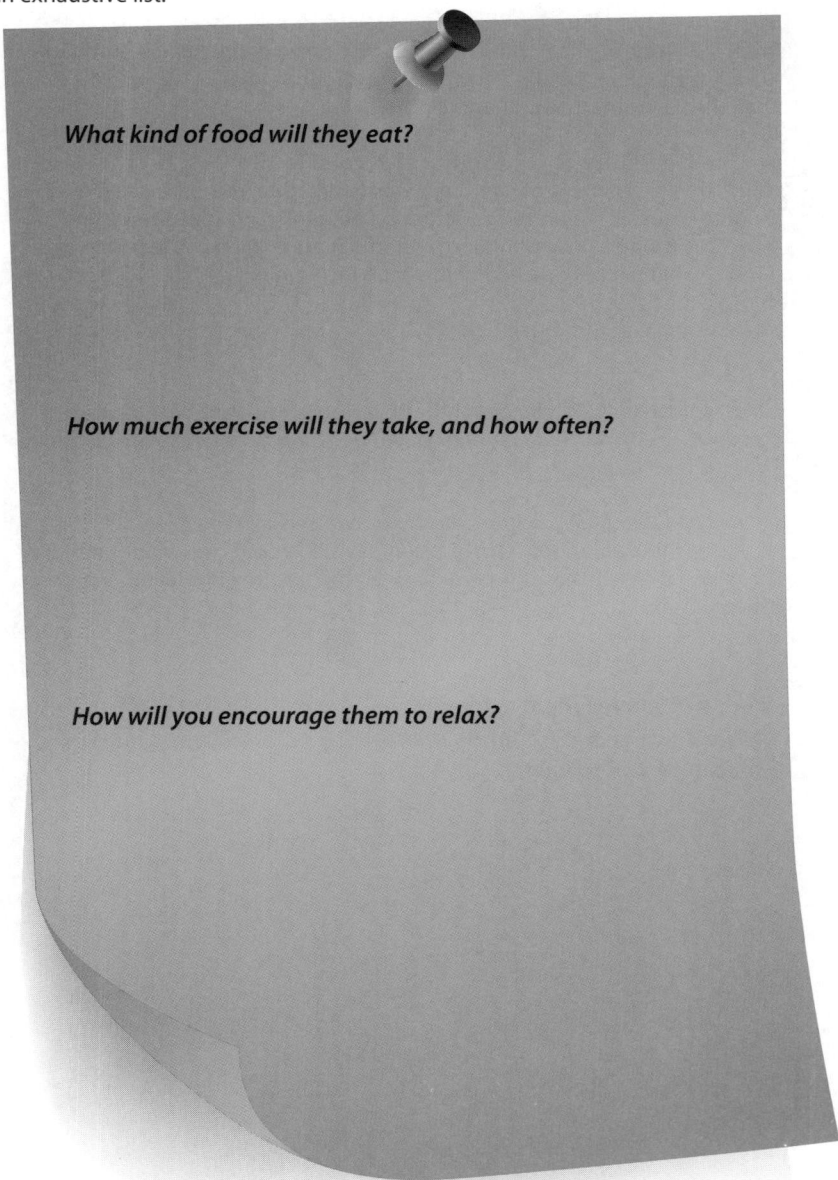

What kind of food will they eat?

How much exercise will they take, and how often?

How will you encourage them to relax?

Colour In Your Future... **FINDING THE REAL YOU**

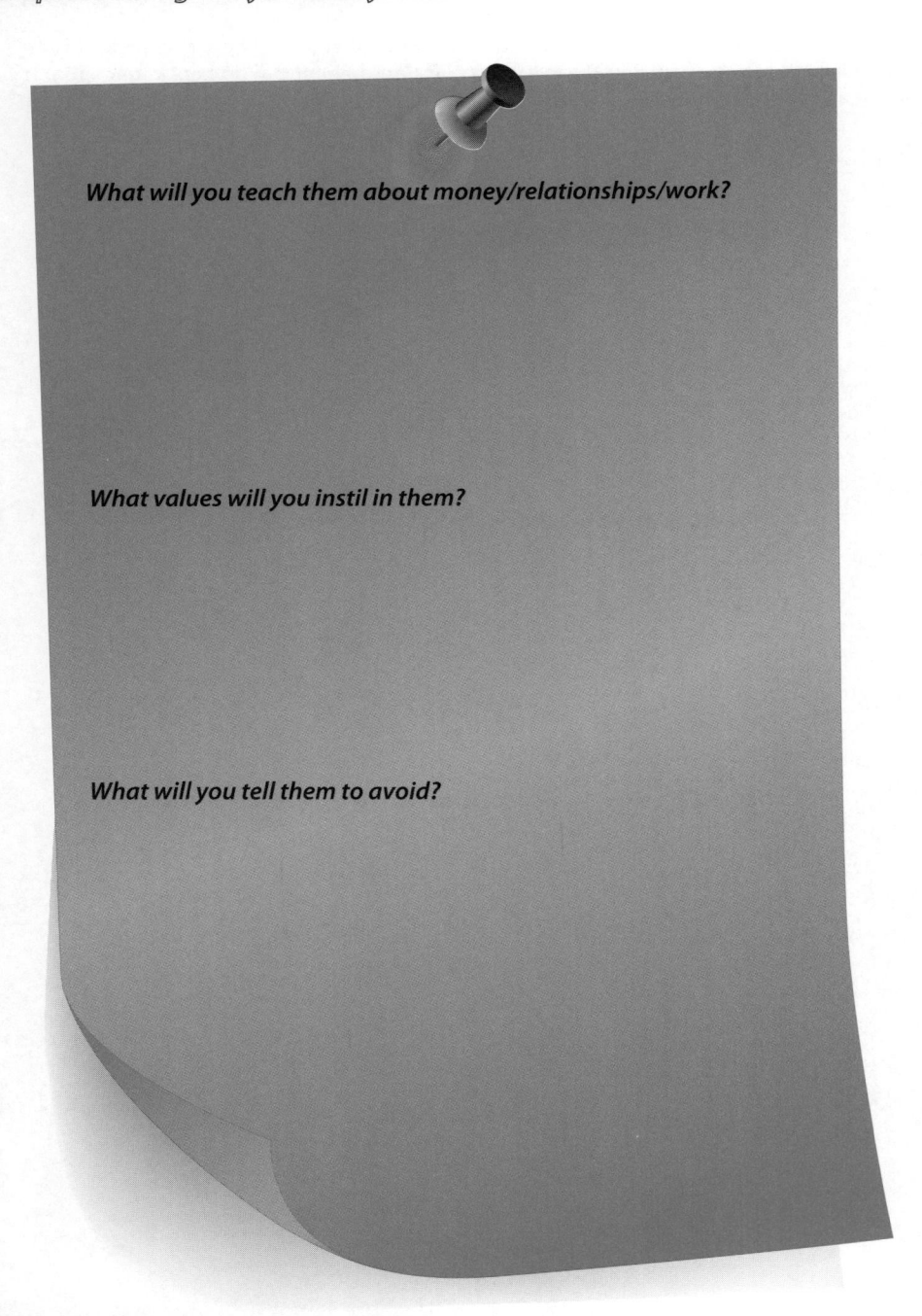

Chapter 6: Living as if you value yourself

What will you teach them about money/relationships/work?

What values will you instil in them?

What will you tell them to avoid?

Chapter 6: Living as if you value yourself

Once you've completed the list to your satisfaction, note which of those things you do for yourself. If you don't do many of them, answer the following question.

What is stopping me from living as if I value myself?

Chapter 6: Living as if you value yourself

Regardless of your answer to the previous question, now you can make a positive choice to change the way you have been living. I'm not saying that your answer is unimportant – it may be hugely significant and have a real bearing on who you are and how you live your life. If that is the case, then you may feel that it's something you want to work through with a coach.

To start making that change, choose two or three things from your list that you feel would be easy to achieve, and note them down:

1.

2.

3.

What habits will you need to change?

Chapter 6: Living as if you value yourself

What new assumptions will you need to make?

Which of your values will you be serving by doing this?

Colour In Your Future... **FINDING THE REAL YOU**

Chapter 6: Living as if you value yourself

What impact will these changes have on you and those around you?

What difference will it make to how you feel about yourself when your changes start to take effect?

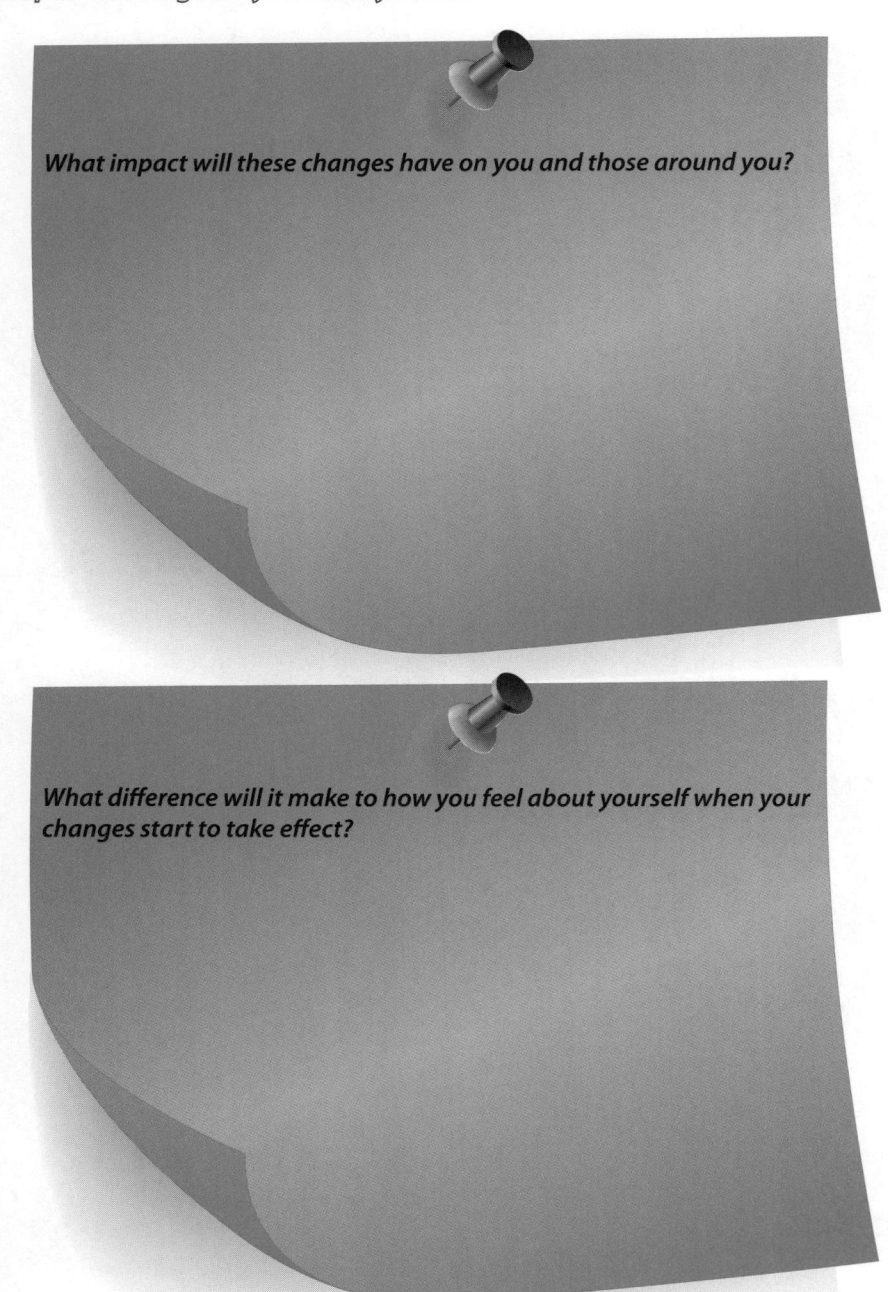

Chapter 7
Getting rid of your Gremlins

Chapter 7: Getting rid of your Gremlins

Do you ever get the feeling that you are sabotaging yourself? It's a cliché to say 'the only person that stops me from doing things is me', but clichés come into being precisely because they are so true. This chapter is all about identifying the things we do that get in our way and stop us from doing what we need to do.

Each of us has our own set of internal would-be helpers that somehow have gone to the 'Dark Side'. We innately desire to do whatever we can to make ourselves feel good, and our brains supply us with lots of ways to do that. The most striking example of this is seen in people who have undergone a major trauma. If the brain decides that the memory of the event would be too hard to handle, it simply erases it, thus protecting itself from further trauma.

Similarly, our internal helpers are constantly looking for other ways to make us feel good about ourselves, to the extent that many people believe that every action we take has some kind of positive intent behind it. Think about it for a moment.

> "Every single thing that you do has a positive intent behind it, which means that every single thing that everyone does has a positive intent behind it".

At this point, most people automatically think: 'But what about murderers or arsonists?' To the outside observer, there doesn't appear to be anything very positive about murder or arson, but what those people are forgetting is that the action is designed to make the person carrying it out feel good or better about themselves. Something within the arsonist or murderer is gratified by those actions, regardless of the impact that they may have on others (or possibly precisely because of their impact on others). The fact that their actions may go against society's moral codes is neither here nor there.

Now, thankfully most of us are not murderers or arsonists, but everything we do still has a positive intent. However, sometimes this becomes skewed and we end up sabotaging ourselves in our attempts to do ourselves good. This is because our internal helpers have become Gremlins and are trying too hard or are jumping in when it's inappropriate.

For example, think of a boy scout helping old ladies across the road. It's all well and good – until he insists on helping old ladies across the road when they don't want to go.

> To help you out, here are some examples of common Gremlins.
> - **Ms Purr Fection** won't let you rest until everything is absolutely 100 per cent perfect, whether it needs to be or not. Unfortunately, she has no clear idea of what she means by perfect – just that whatever you do, it isn't perfect.
> - **Mr Can't B. Arsed** would rather encourage you to slump on the sofa and not make any effort than have you get your teeth stuck into a challenge.
> - **Mr Realmen** will tell you that 'real men' enjoy football and drink 10 pints a night, so you can't be one if you prefer a good book and a nice cup of tea.

Chapter 7: Getting rid of your Gremlins

- **Ms Ima Fatpig** constantly berates you for not being a size 8 and insists that you will never be happy until you lose 4st.

You can tell when your Gremlins are around because you'll hear them whispering to you via your inner voice – you may have met them already in Chapter 4. They can arrive on their own, or they can come en masse when you're feeling vulnerable. You might know already what the signs are, telling them that now's a good time to call.

However, the thing to remember is that these Gremlins do have a positive intention. They may be expressing their dissatisfaction with you as you are in this moment, but really they do want the best for you – it's just that they are going about it in the wrong way, just like that boy scout.

So, how can you spot these Gremlins, and what can you do to get them to become helpful again? This next exercise will show you.

Exercise
Take some time to think about what your Gremlins might be. Give them silly names like the ones above. Draw cartoons or caricatures of them. They don't have to be perfect, but making fun of them starts to make them less scary and reduces their impact.

My Gremlin Name

Picture

Colour In Your Future... **FINDING THE REAL YOU**

Chapter 7: Getting rid of your Gremlins

What is this Gremlin telling me?

When does it visit me?

Now think about what needs to happen to reduce the impact of each Gremlin. As an example, Mr Can't B. Arsed is one of mine, and I drew him as a big, bloated ball of hot air and noxious gasses. I realised it would only take one small pinprick to make him shrivel up and disappear, and that one realisation instantly made him much less powerful and significant.

Chapter 7: Getting rid of your Gremlins

How can you reduce the impact of your Gremlins?

Once you've seen that it's possible to reduce your Gremlins to a state of insignificance, it's time to start thinking about what they are really trying to do. Have a dialogue with each Gremlin, and ask it what its positive intention is. Once you know that, you can tell it how you would really like to be helped.

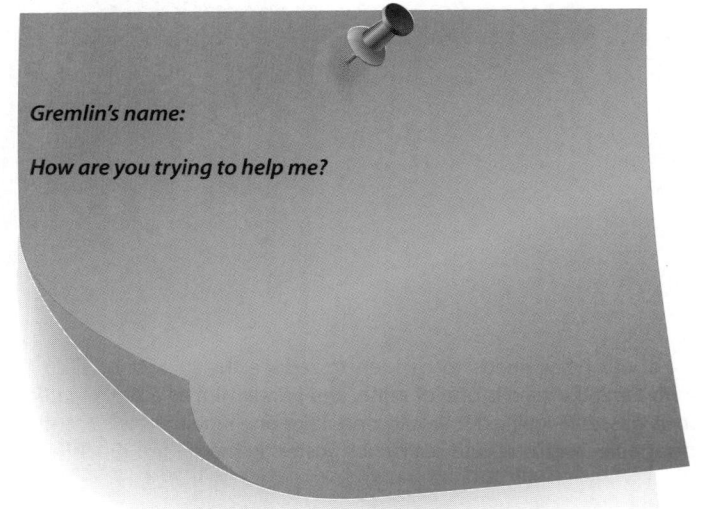

Gremlin's name:

How are you trying to help me?

Chapter 7: Getting rid of your Gremlins

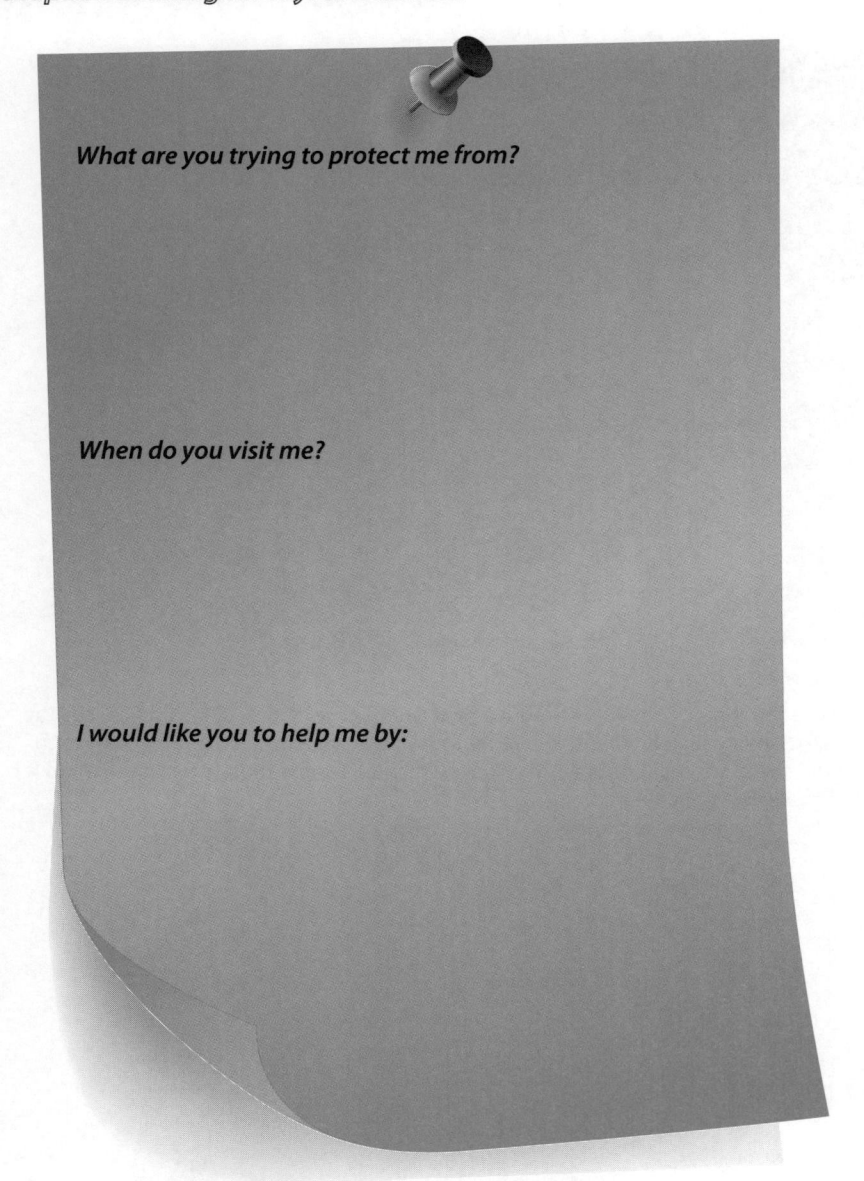

What are you trying to protect me from?

When do you visit me?

I would like you to help me by:

Once you have answers to these questions, you'll find that the next time your Gremlin arrives, you can choose not to do what it says and not to get angry with it. Rather, you'll be able to remind yourself of its positive intentions and then think through the situation you're faced with in that moment to see how it can help you, rather than allowing it to sabotage your progress.

Chapter 8
Blibbles

Chapter 8: Blibbles

'Blibbles' is the name I've given to the Gremlins that haven't gone to the 'Dark Side' – they are the inner voices that are helpful and lead you into positive behaviours.

> **Here are my top three Blibbles.**
>
> - **Happy Blibble** – is on a bouncy castle. She is exuberant, childlike, excitable and enthusiastic, and loves to encourage playfulness in others. Every time she bounces, she sees the world from a new and different perspective, and that leads her to all sorts of new ideas and new discoveries.
>
> - **Loving Blibble** – is carrying a huge platter of food that she has just prepared specifically to nurture those around her. She is warm, affectionate and generous and takes great pleasure in the successes and triumphs of those around her.
>
> - **Intrepid Blibble** – wears a pith helmet and carries a machete so that he can slash through the jungly undergrowth, making new paths for himself and the ones that come behind him. He is bold, brave and questing.

I believe that we all have these positive voices in our heads, but for reasons of modesty or fear of boastfulness, we tend to dismiss or ignore them. This is not to say that we don't take note of what they say, but that rather than celebrating them and being glad to have them around, we take them for granted and can be dismissive of their positive effect on us and those around us.

It seems daft to me that we spend time agonising or feeling guilty over the negative things we tell ourselves, while dismissing or making light of the positive things, so this next set of questions is designed to help you to celebrate your Blibbles. Just as you did with your Gremlins, take some time to think about what your Blibbles might be. Give them silly names like the ones above. Draw cartoons or caricatures of them. They don't have to be perfect, but instead of making fun of them, this time try to describe them with love.

My Blibble Name

Picture

Chapter 8: Blibbles

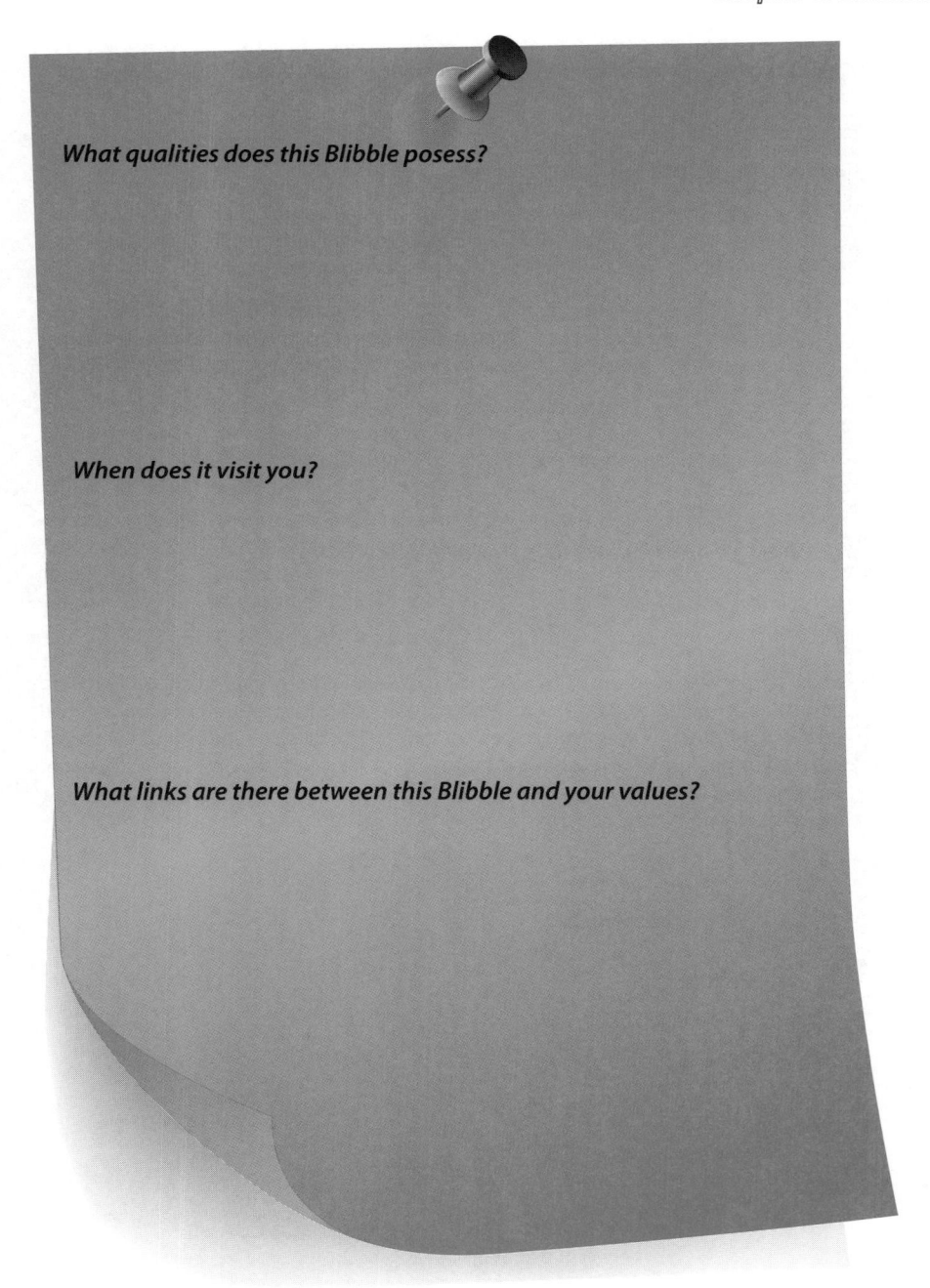

What qualities does this Blibble posess?

When does it visit you?

What links are there between this Blibble and your values?

Chapter 8: Blibbles

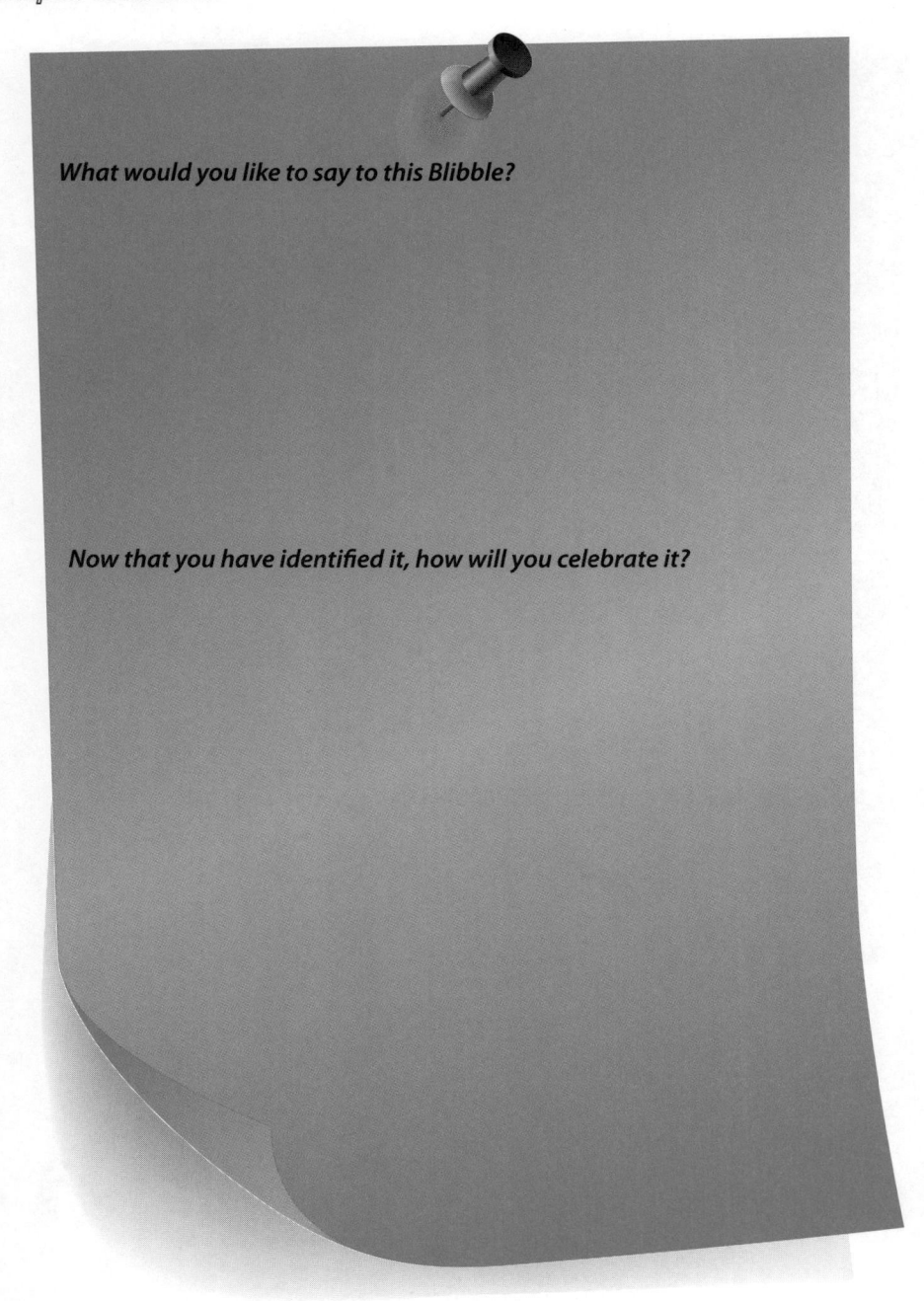

What would you like to say to this Blibble?

Now that you have identified it, how will you celebrate it?

Chapter 9
Why are other people so weird?

Chapter 9: Why are other people so weird?

No matter how long you've been at university, no doubt you will have come across a fair number of really weird people. They may be fellow students, faculty members or locals that you've met since moving from home, and their degrees of weirdness will have varied. You may have known some pretty weird people at home and school too, but they will have been familiar to you, and familiarity lessens the impact of weirdness.

Now here you are in this unfamiliar environment, with none of your support structures, seemingly surrounded by weirdos. Some people don't appear to be weird at the start, and it is only after they've lulled you into a false sense of security that you realise that all is not as it seemed. Others appear to be weird from the outset and you are likely to have given them a wide berth. Others still may have seemed weird at the start, but have become normal as you have come to know them. In the back of your mind, there lurks the unspoken fear: am I weird too? And if I am weird, am I the only person who can't tell?

Here's the thing: unless there is something clinically wrong with their mental health (and I'm talking psychosis of some sort here), these people aren't weird – they're just different. There are an infinite number of ways of being a healthy, happy, functioning human being, and every time someone is born, another new way of being is born along with them.

The more different to you a person is, the more likely you are to find them weird, unsettling, difficult, challenging, etc. The more like you they are, the more you'll find them companionable, easy going, attractive and fun to be with – unless they're very much like you and share some of your worst traits when, strangely, you can find them deeply annoying! This is because they're a constant reminder to you of your worst bits, and, let's face it, who wants to be reminded of those?

We get used to seeing the world through our own eyes and with the benefit of our own experiences. We become familiar with the way that we do things, and with the reasons why we do things. So when we see someone else behaving in a particular way, we think about what would make us behave in that way and assume that the other person is doing so for the same reason as us.

The mistake we make when we do this is forgetting that the other person has had a completely different life to us, so they are very unlikely to have the same motivations, beliefs, background and opinions as we do. So when we see people doing things that we think are weird or stupid or unpleasant, we jump to conclusions about why they are behaving that way, and treat them accordingly.

What is more helpful – for us and for them – is to learn to think of all the reasons why they could be behaving in that way, and then try to find out which one is right. Often you'll find that people's intentions are far more positive than you had thought at first, and they are unaware of the impact that their behaviour is having.

Chapter 9: Why are other people so weird?

A key thing to remember is the concept of positive intent that we covered in Chapter 7: remembering this when you observe other people's behaviour can be really useful. It encourages you to think objectively, so rather than finding yourself becoming annoyed, fearful or cynical about someone else's behaviour, you'll find yourself mentally running through all of the reasons that could lie behind it, which will automatically help you to become more forgiving of other people. It also helps you to become more forgiving of yourself, as one of the by-products of this type of thinking is a growing awareness of your own motivations.

The following exercise is designed to help you to think about what might be going on for all of those weirdos out there... including you!

Exercise

Call to mind everyone that strikes you as a weirdo and write down what it is about them that makes them weird in your eyes: clothes, habits, behaviour, interests, personal characteristics – whatever that may be.

What similarities are there between all the people that you find weird?

Chapter 9: Why are other people so weird?

Think back to the work that we did on values. Do any of the 'weird' characteristics that you've noted down go against any of your values?

What feelings do these elements of 'weirdness' evoke in you? What fears are lurking there? (Be honest with yourself.)

Pick one of the 'weird' people on your list and try to put yourself in their shoes. If you were them, what might lie behind your behaviour, appearance or characteristics? Remember to bear in mind the idea of positive intent.

Chapter 9: Why are other people so weird?

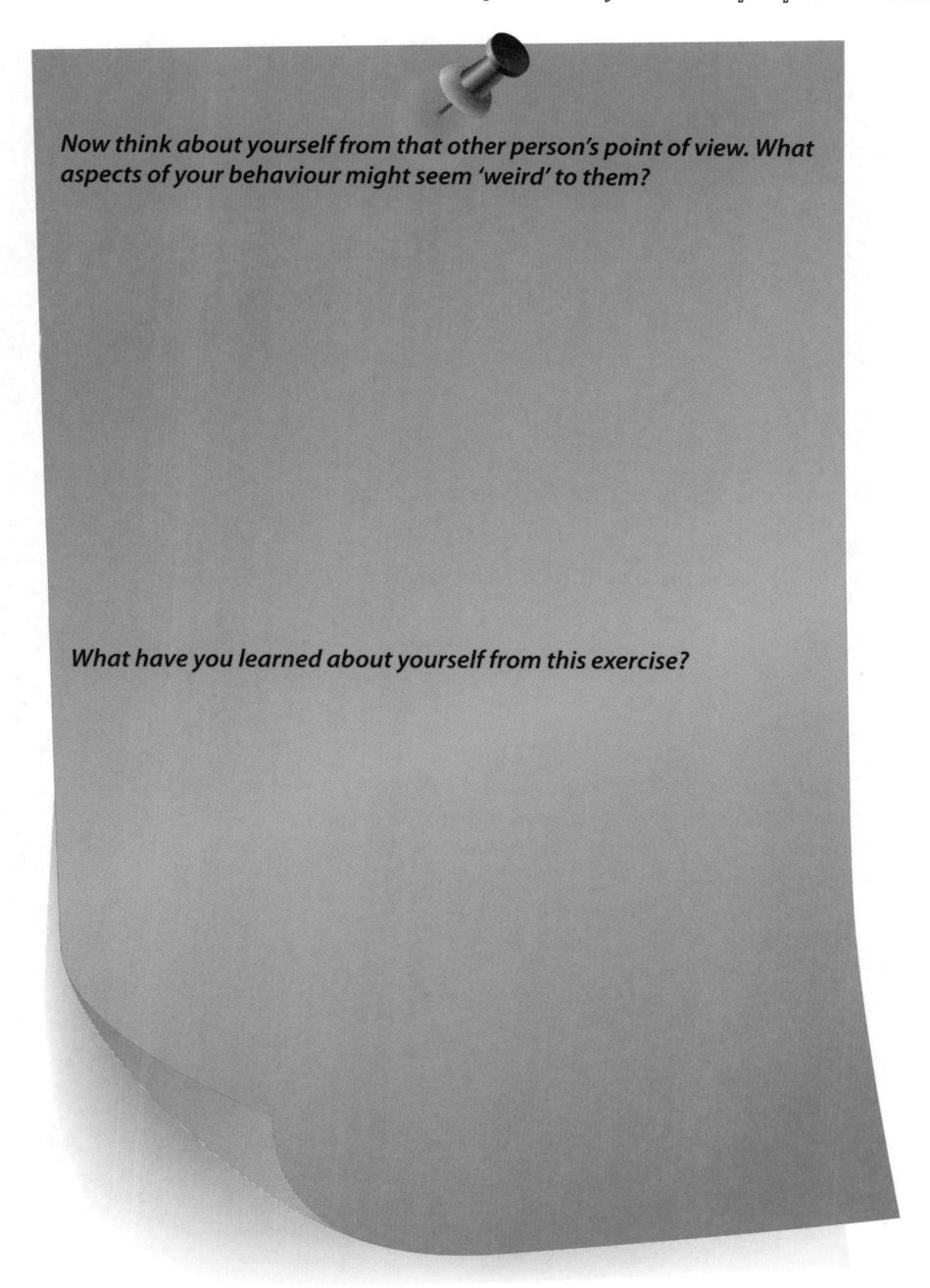

Now think about yourself from that other person's point of view. What aspects of your behaviour might seem 'weird' to them?

What have you learned about yourself from this exercise?

Chapter 9: Why are other people so weird?

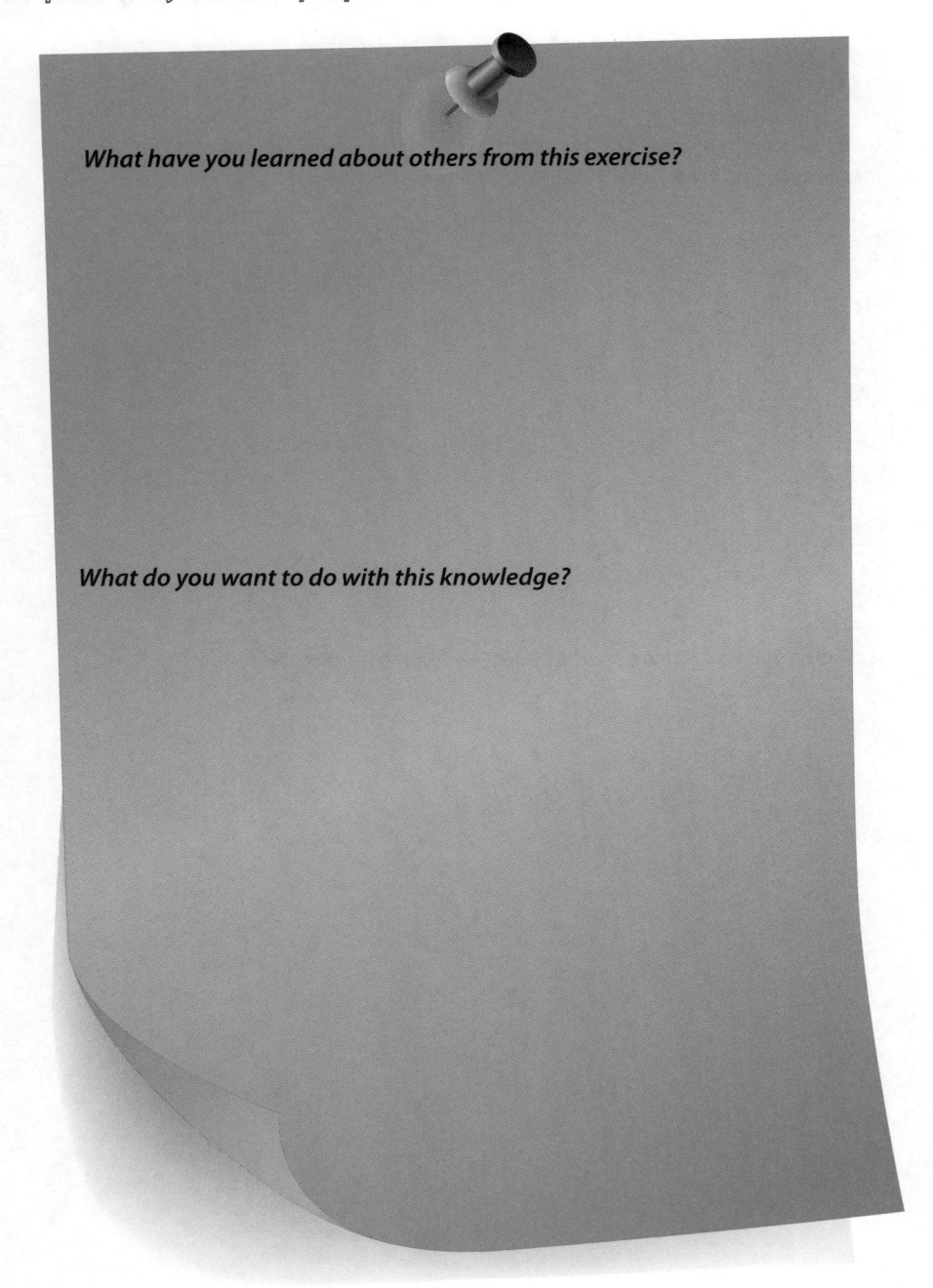

What have you learned about others from this exercise?

What do you want to do with this knowledge?

Chapter 10
I'm OK, you're OK

Chapter 10: I'm OK, you're OK

Have you noticed how easy some people find it to say the right thing at the right time to the right person, and how other people seem to find it just as easy to mess up every time?

When you are in a new place, surrounded by strangers and out of your comfort zone, it can be especially hard to relax and go with the flow, and lots of us end up either staying silent or talking too much because we're trying too hard.

On top of all that, we've already looked at the way that, when you get to university, people suddenly start treating you like an adult and expecting you to behave like one. Again, some people take to it like a duck to water, and some take years to get used to even thinking of themselves as an adult, let alone behaving like one. Then there are the people who have convinced themselves that they've got it sorted, while the rest of the world observes them going out and alienating people left, right and centre.

So much of this is down to the attitude that you take, both to yourself and other people. If you constantly assume that you're fantastic and everyone else is a waste of good skin, then you're going to project that attitude in your dealings with them. You'll become critical of others and find ways to blame them when things go wrong, ignoring any contribution you may have made. Often people become like this as a way of covering up their own insecurities and end up being perceived as arrogant.

If your attitude is that you're hopeless and everyone around you is hopeless, then you're beaten before you even begin. Your world view is likely to be 'Why bother? It'll never do any good' – and you'll prove yourself right time and time again.

If you think that it's just you who is useless and everyone else is much better than you, then you'll be spending all your time beating yourself up and desperately trying to win approval from those around you. You may well come across as desperate to please, and some people will take advantage of that.

Ideally, your attitude will be that you're OK, and the people around you are OK. You're on an equal footing and, in that frame of mind, you can work cooperatively to get things done.

This diagram shows these four attitudes.

I'm OK, you're OK	I'm OK, you're not OK
Gets on with	Gets rid of
Optimistic, healthy outlook	Critical and mistrustful, lacks insight into self
Balanced relationships	Anger and frustration
Problem solver	Blames others

Chapter 10: I'm OK, you're OK

I'm not OK, you're OK	I'm not OK, you're not OK
Gets away from	Gets nowhere with
Looks for approval, undervalues self	Often doesn't bother, beaten before begins
Inadequacy, guilt, fear	Despair, rejection
Blames self	Blames everyone

This exercise aims to help you identify which attitude you use most commonly, and to think about how you'd like to change your attitude, if you wish to.

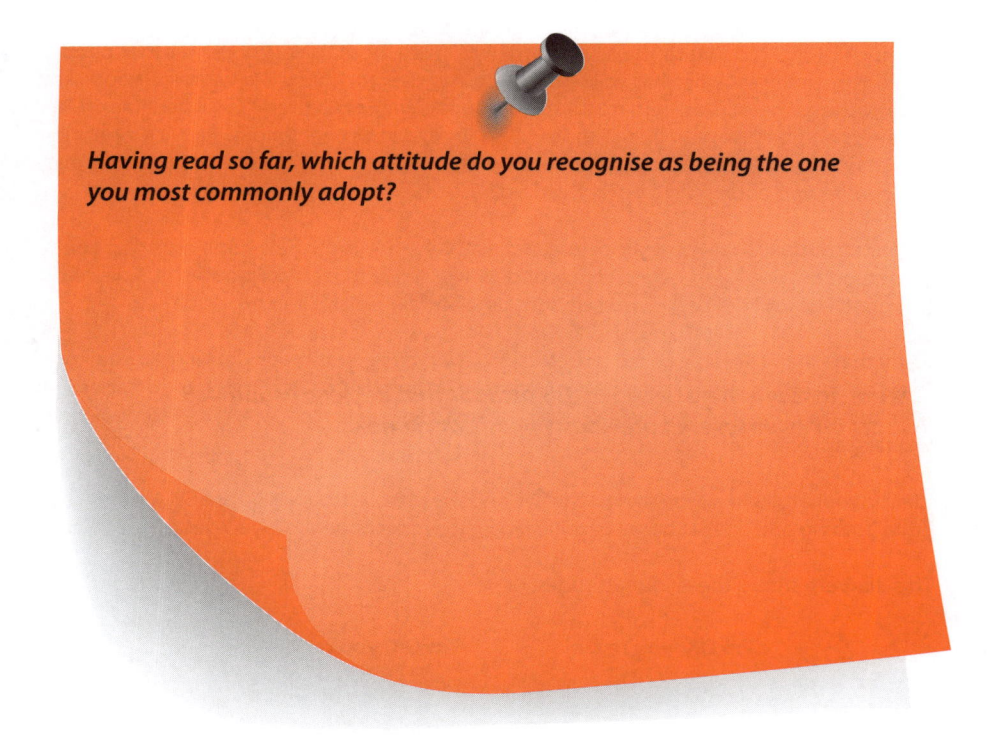

Having read so far, which attitude do you recognise as being the one you most commonly adopt?

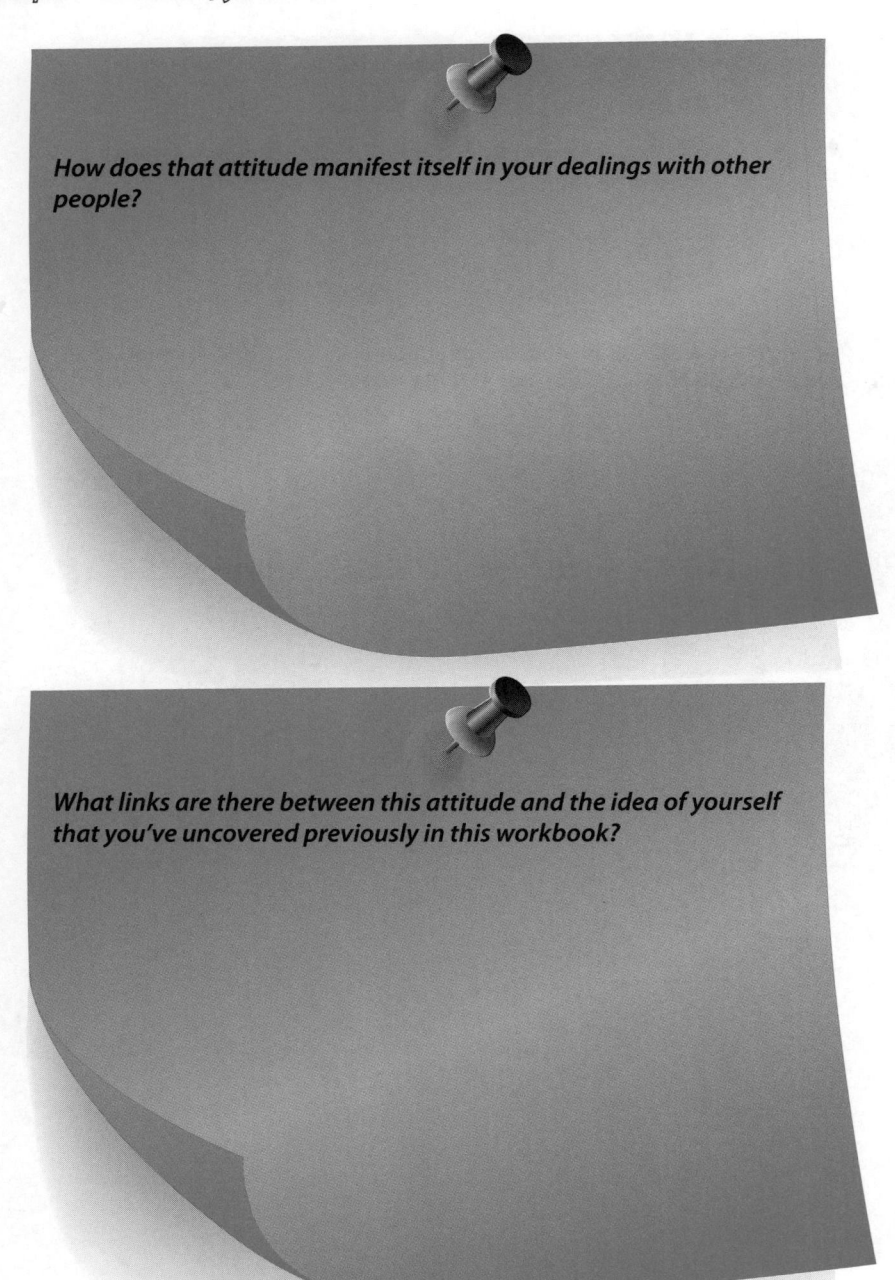

Chapter 10: I'm OK, you're OK

How does that attitude manifest itself in your dealings with other people?

What links are there between this attitude and the idea of yourself that you've uncovered previously in this workbook?

Chapter 10: I'm OK, you're OK

How can the work that you've done so far help you to develop a more helpful attitude towards yourself and others?

Chapter 11
Daring to dream

Chapter 11: Daring to dream

Remember when you were a child, and you had no concept of what you could or couldn't achieve? Back then, it was perfectly possible for you to grow up and become an engine driver or World Cup footballer, a lion tamer or a princess, an astronaut or a doctor or a film star, or whatever else it was that you dreamed of. The first exercise in this book will have helped you to get back in touch with that child, and made you aware of how much your life now differs from the life you dreamed of having all those years ago. So what happened?

As you got older, you will have absorbed ideas and preconceptions from other people that will have had an effect on how you viewed those childhood dreams. You may have been told that they were unrealistic or 'not for the likes of us'. You may have been told that you weren't clever enough or that only boys or girls did that kind of job – or even that it wasn't a real job and you should be more serious. Over the years our need to conform to what other people expect of us takes a stronger hold, and we end up doing things that would have made our younger selves howl with disappointment.

So many of us reach adulthood and find ourselves living a life that (hopefully) pays the bills and allows us to provide for ourselves and our families, but leaves an unfulfilled place inside of us. Often we choose to ignore that place out of fear of what might happen if we examined it too closely. We tell ourselves that our dreams are unrealistic, that this is real life and we should just put our head down and get on with it, regardless of how unfulfilled we feel.

This is a process that can start very early. Even now, you may be studying a subject because it's sensible and will lead to a good career, but which doesn't fulfil you. You may have sublimated a passion for art, music, geography or history because parental pressure or your own lack of self-confidence has convinced you that the sensible approach is best.

I believe very passionately that life doesn't have to be that way, and that you have the right to develop your potential and show the world your true colours. I'm living proof. For years I wanted to work for myself but thought that people who did that were somehow special, and that there was no way I could ever be like them. However, I came to realise that these people weren't so different from me after all, and that the only thing stopping me from making my dream a reality was me.

That moment of realisation lead me to end a 25-year career with the same employer and start my own business doing what I love and what I believe I was put on this earth to do. Something that I had thought of for years as a pipe dream has become a reality. I've welcomed in a whole new me, and my life has been enriched as a result. I don't want you to have to wait that long to live the life you want and deserve.

Chapter 11: Daring to dream

Do you have a secret dream? Is there something that you want to achieve in your life that you're telling yourself is unrealistic or unobtainable for some reason? Provided that the goal is within your control, there is no reason why you shouldn't be able to achieve it.

Winning the lottery isn't within your control – buying a ticket will at least put you in the game, but it won't significantly raise your chances of success. However, learning to play the violin is entirely within your grasp, as is writing that novel, setting up your own business, learning to speak Chinese or losing weight. There's also no reason why you shouldn't become a lion tamer, doctor, engine driver or even an astronaut if that's what you really want. (Becoming a princess might be more problematic and is possibly not entirely within your control, but you never know!)

If you're serious about wanting to achieve your goal, start by writing it down. It's been proven that people who write their goals down are far more likely to achieve them than people who don't, so get yourself a head start. Make sure you write it down in positive terms and put the date by which you want to achieve it. So if you want to learn to play the violin, you might express it like this:

"By the end of 2011, I will have achieved Grade 1 on the violin"

This gives you something concrete to aim for, with a way of measuring how far you've come and in a timeframe that sounds realistic to you.

Beware of goals that are expressed in the negative, as they won't get you anywhere. If you express your goal like this:

"I want to stop eating chocolate"

you'll find yourself fixating on chocolate and probably end up eating even more of it. If you express your goal as:

"I will eat five pieces of fruit every day"

your diet will become healthier and you won't be conditioning yourself to think about chocolate all the time.

Obviously there is more to achieving a goal than just writing it down, but you'll be amazed at the difference it makes.

Chapter 11: Daring to dream

My goal is:

Signature: .... Date: ....

Colour In Your Future... **FINDING THE REAL YOU**

Take the certificate out of this workbook and put it up on the wall so you can look at it every day.

Read it out loud to yourself.

Get your friends and family to support you by asking how it's going.

Bring it to life.

There is no reason why your secret dream has to remain a secret any more. The more you think about it and talk about it, the more achieving it becomes a part of your everyday reality. You'll be amazed at how many opportunities come your way. It will seem as if the universe is trying to help you, and if you're serious about achieving it, you'll find yourself at a point where it's impossible to remember that you ever thought that your goal was unrealistic.

Chapter 12
Colouring in your future

Chapter 12: Colouring in your future

So here you are at the end of the book, but the start of your journey. This is where you take everything you have learned and discovered about yourself, and decide what to do about it.

If you have worked through each chapter in order, you will have amassed a huge amount of data about yourself and what makes you tick. I hope you also will have some pretty clear ideas of what you want to have different in your life from this point onwards.

Now is the point at which you have to decide whether or not to commit to making your life different. The choice is yours alone. No one else can make it for you and only you know what changes are right for you. The following questions are designed to help you to ensure that, whatever goals you set yourself, you've thoroughly thought through the implications and are in the best possible place to achieve them.

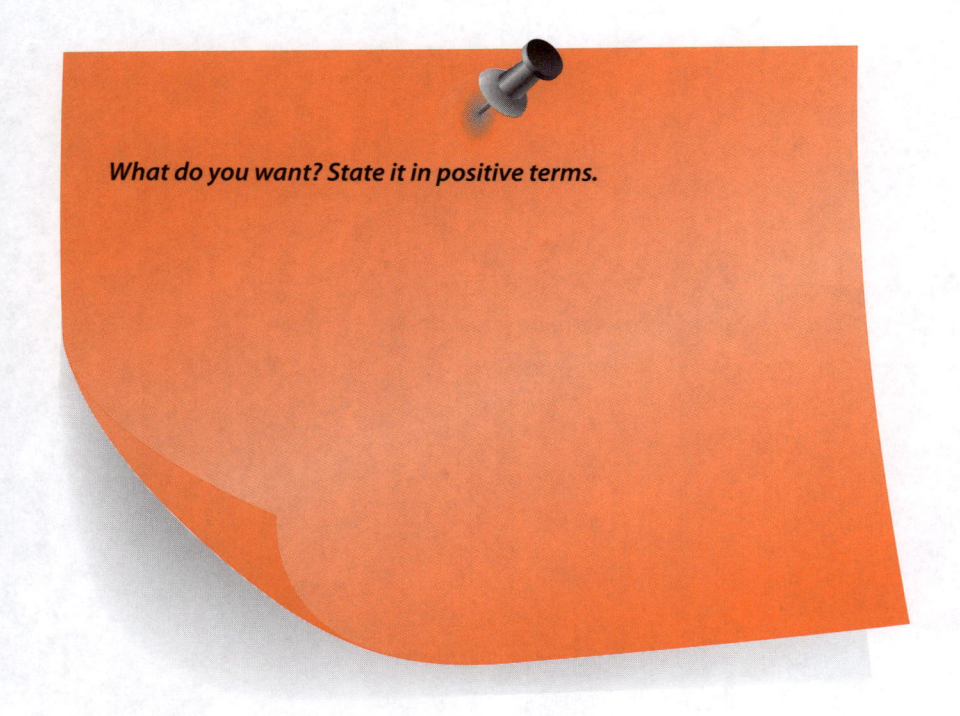

What do you want? State it in positive terms.

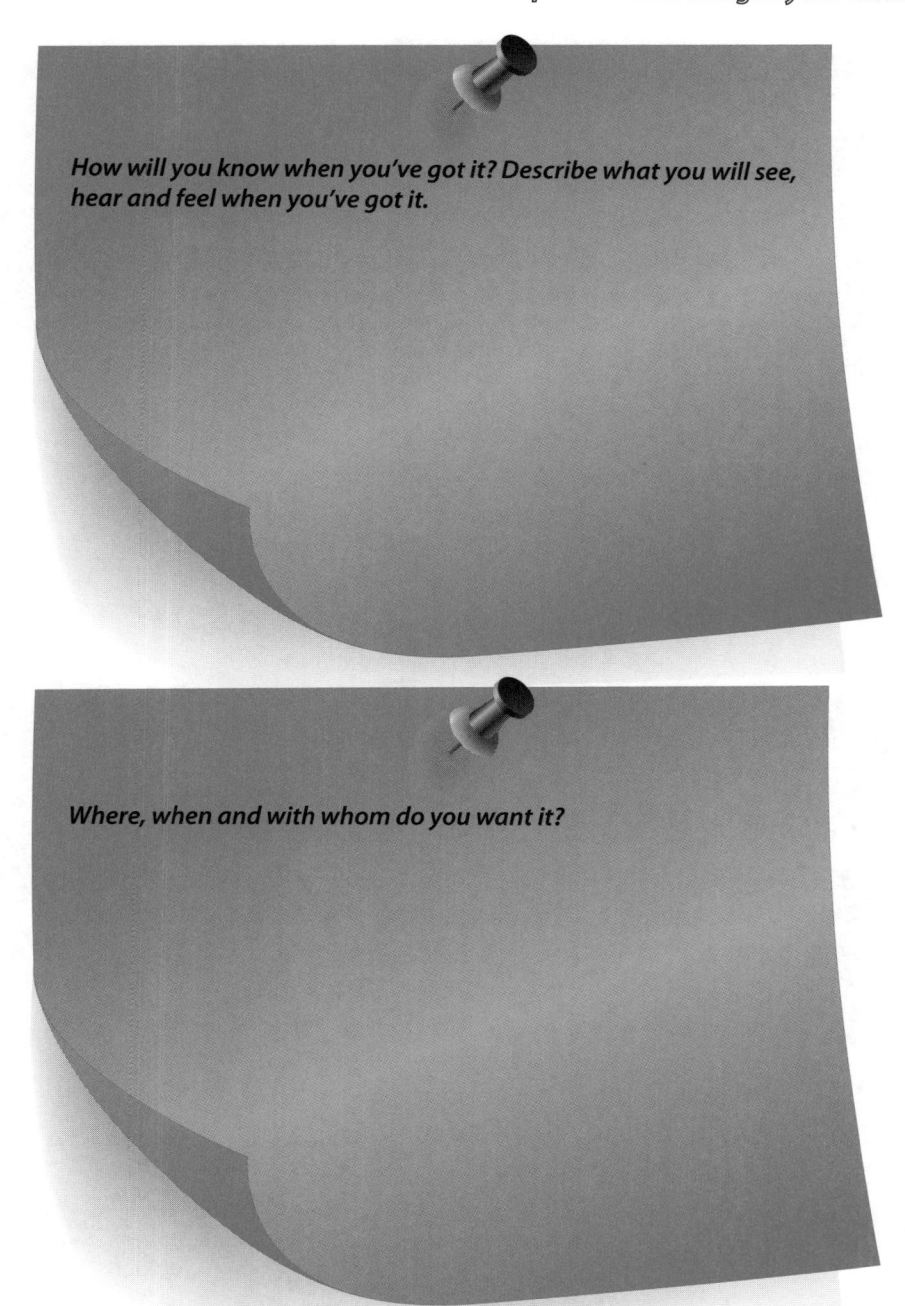

Chapter 12: Colouring in your future

How will you know when you've got it? Describe what you will see, hear and feel when you've got it.

Where, when and with whom do you want it?

Colour In Your Future... FINDING THE REAL YOU

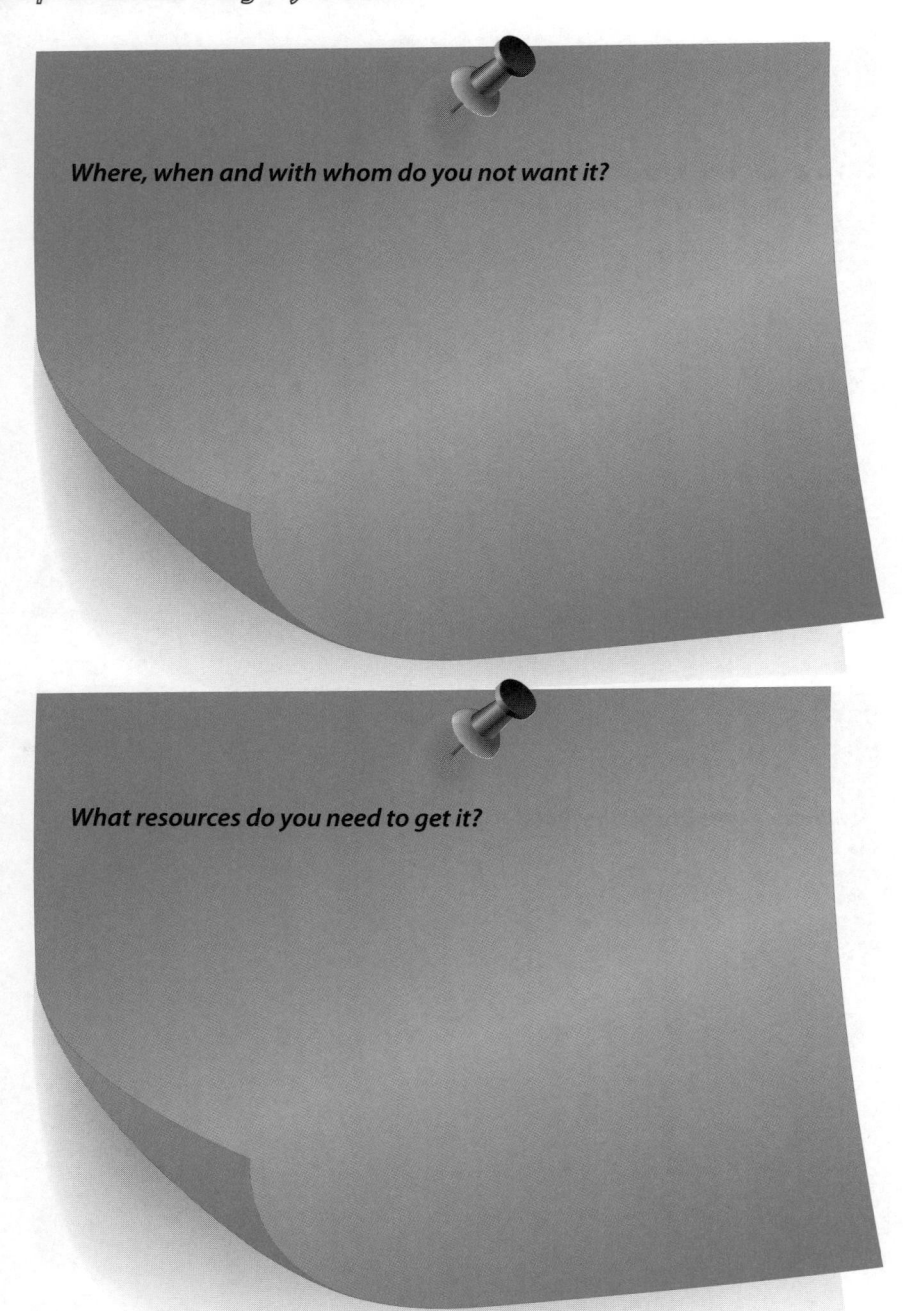

Chapter 12: Colouring in your future

Where, when and with whom do you not want it?

What resources do you need to get it?

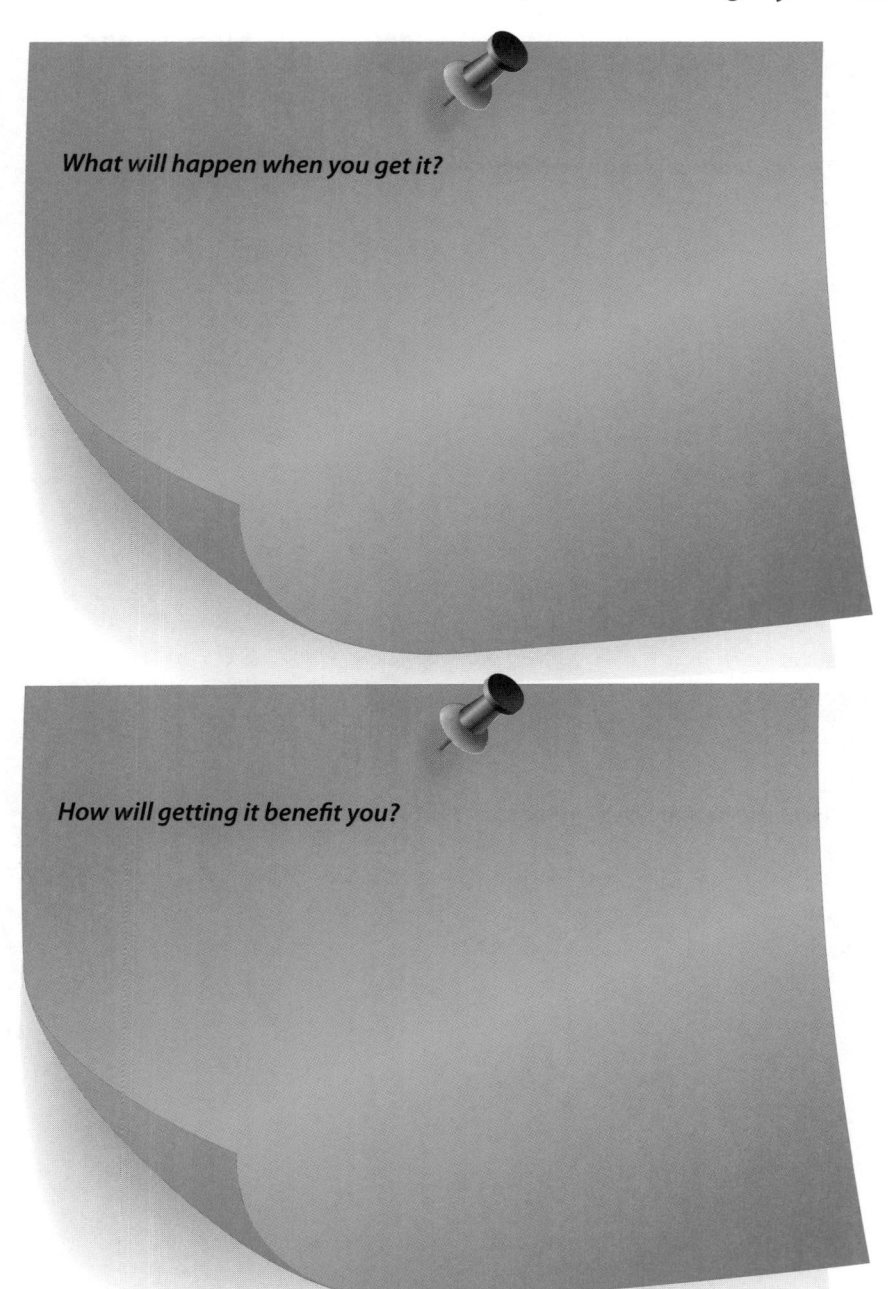

Chapter 12: Colouring in your future

What will happen when you get it?

How will getting it benefit you?

Chapter 12: Colouring in your future

Do you want this change in any other situation?

How will making this change affect other aspects of your life?

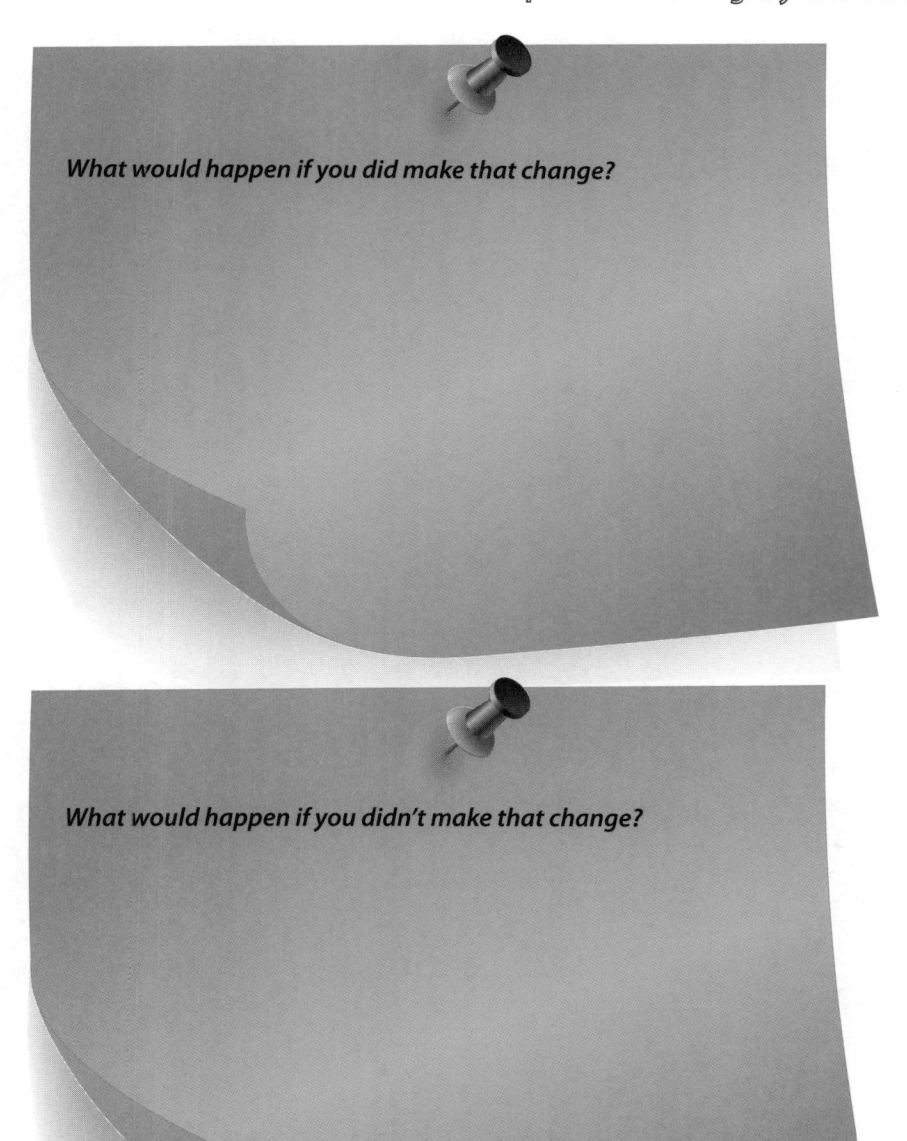

Chapter 12: Colouring in your future

What would happen if you did make that change?

What would happen if you didn't make that change?

Colour In Your Future... FINDING THE REAL YOU

Chapter 12: Colouring in your future

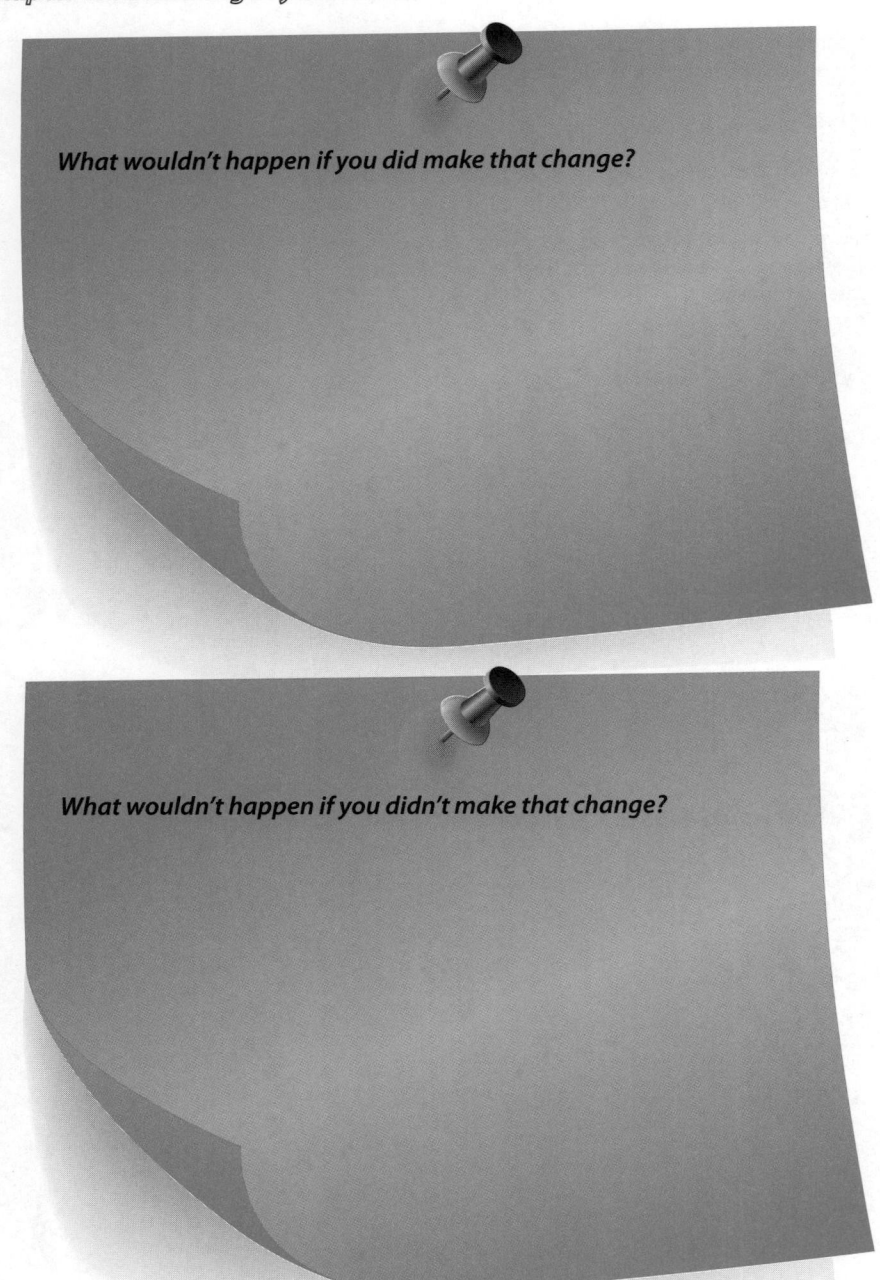

What wouldn't happen if you did make that change?

What wouldn't happen if you didn't make that change?

Chapter 12: Colouring in your future

Think carefully about those last four questions: they're not designed to catch you out, rather to make you really think deeply about your answers.

By the time you have answered every question, you will have a very clear idea of what you want and how you're going to get it. How exciting! Now all you have to do is take your first step.

All that remains is for me to wish you well as you embark on this exciting new period of your life. I hope you enjoy your journey, and I look forward to working with you at some point along the way.

Now go and colour in your future!